Hertfordshire
COUNTY COUNCIL
Community Information

2 0 APR 2001

1 5 MAY 2002

1 4 DEC 2004

STA

Please renew/return this item by the last date shown.

So that your telephone call is charged at local rate, please call the numbers as set out below:

	From Area codes 01923 or 0208:	From the rest of Herts:
Renewals:	01923 471373	01438 737373
Enquiries:	01923 471333	01438 737333
Minicom:	01923 471599	01438 737599

L32

uncovered editions

Titles in the series

uncovered editions

THE BRITISH INVASION OF TIBET: COLONEL YOUNGHUSBAND, 1904

⟨⟩

London: The Stationery Office

First published 1904 Cd. 1920
© Crown Copyright

This abridged edition
© The Stationery Office 1999
Reprinted with permission.

ISBN 0 11 702409 0

A CIP catalogue record for this book is available from the
British Library.

Printed in the UK by Biddles Limited, Guildford, Surrey
J93485   C50   11/99

Uncovered Editions are historic official papers which have not previously been available in a popular form. The series has been created directly from the archive of The Stationery Office in London, and the books have been chosen for the quality of their story telling. Some subjects are familiar, but others are less well known. Each is a moment of history.

∞◦◦⟨⟩◦◦∞

Temperature

°F		°C	
75	=	23.8	
70	=	21.1	
65	=	18.3	
60	=	15.5	
55	=	12.7	
50	=	10	
45	=	7.2	
40	=	4.4	
35	=	1.6	
32	**=**	**0**	
30	=	-1.1	
25	=	-3.8	
20	=	-6.6	
15	=	-9.4	
10	=	-12.2	
5	=	-15	
0	*=*	*-17.7*	*Degrees*
-5	*=*	*-20.5*	*of frost*
-10	*=*	*-23.3*	
-15	*=*	*-26.1*	
-20	*=*	*-28.8*	
-25	*=*	*-31.6*	
-30	*=*	*-34.4*	
-35	*=*	*-37.2*	
-40	*=*	*-40*	

❦

In 1903, a British Missionary Force under the
Leadership of Colonel Francis Younghusband
crossed over the border from India and invaded
Tibet. This is the account of his actions.

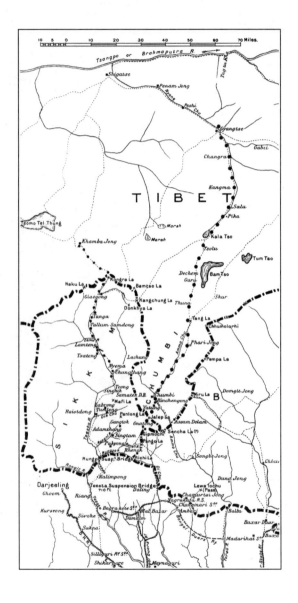

∞◦◊◦∞

From Colonel F. E. Younghusband, C.I.E., Khamba Jong, to the Foreign Secretary, Simla, dated Khamba Jong, the 19th (despatched from Gangtok on 23rd) July, 1903. (Telegraphic.)

I arrived here yesterday.

Letter from the Under-Secretary to the Government of India in the Foreign Department, to Colonel F. E. Younghusband, C.I.E., British Commissioner, Tibet Frontier Commission, dated Simla, the 26th July, 1903.

I am directed to acknowledge the receipt of your letter, dated the 14th July, 1903, forwarding copy of a letter which you have addressed to the Chinese Resident at Lhasa.

In the event of your meeting the Dalai Lama, the Government of India authorise you to give him the assurance which you suggest in your letter.

From Colonel F. E. Younghusband, C.I.E., Khamba Jong, to the Foreign Secretary, Simla, dated Khamba Jong, the 22nd (despatched from Gangtok on 25th) July, 1903. (Telegraphic.)

Amban's reply has been sent to Parr, who is ill at Yatung. I have had two interviews with the Chinese and Tibetan delegates, and am of opinion with White that neither the Chinese nor Tibetans have sufficient position or influence. The Tibetans said they could not even report to their Government the substance of a speech I made, and refused to accept a copy of it, which Mr. Ho's Secretary suggested I should give them, and which, with Mr. Ho's approval, I handed over to the Grand Secretary.

From Colonel F. E. Younghusband, C.I.E., Khamba Jong, to the Foreign Secretary, Simla, dated Khamba Jong, the 23rd (despatched from Gangtok on 27th) July, 1903. (Telegraphic.)

Note: The Amban is the senior Chinese Official.

Following from Amban Yu to Viceroy has been given to me by Mr. Ho for transmission by telegraph: "From Your Excellency's despatch I learnt you wished me to appoint Commissioners for negotiations. I have sent reply to you, and instructed Captain Parr to translate it and forward it to you immediately. Now I have received petitions from my Deputy, Mr. Ho, that the Commissioners appointed by Your Excellency have arrived at Khamba Jong with soldiers. Tibetan officers are so suspicious that they are not willing to discuss matters. I have informed you in my reply that Khamba Jong is in Tibetan territory and unsuitable for discussion. I now request Your Excellency to issue orders to your Commissioners to remove to the boundary, and then we can easily commence discussion. Your doing this will show friendliness to both countries. So I hope you will do it, and reply soon by telegram."

Before replying to above, please await arrival of my letter of 22nd July.

Letter from Colonel F. E. Younghusband, C.I.E., British Commissioner, Tibet Frontier Commission, to the Secretary to the Government of India in the Foreign Department, dated Khamba Jong, the 22nd July, 1903.
(Extract.)

I have the honour to report, for the information of the Government of India, that on 20th July I paid a visit to Mr. Ho who, with the Tibetan Grand Secretary, received me in a tent. Mr. Ho is not a very polished official and did not favorably impress me. The Grand Secretary, on the other hand, has an exceedingly genial, kind, accomplished style of face, and looked very like any monk of that description you might see in Europe. He seems, however, to have very little power or influence. After the usual compliments, Mr. Ho said that the Viceroy had fixed upon this place for the negotiations : but it was not at all a suitable place, especially if the negotiations lasted any time as they were very likely to. I said that the Viceroy had selected Khamaba Jong because of its proximity to the frontier, and I added that His Excellency chose a place on the Tibetan rather than on the Indian side of the frontier because the last negotiations were conducted in India, and when after much trouble a Treaty was concluded between the Chinese and the British Governments, the Tibetans had repudiated it, saying they knew nothing about it. On the present occasion, therefore, the Viceroy decided that the negotiations should take place in Tibet, and His Excellency asked that a Tibetan official of the highest rank should take part in them, in order that, when the new settlement was completed, the Tibetans should not be able to say they knew nothing of it. Mr. Ho said, he hoped, we would settle everything in a friendly manner. I replied that I saw no reason why we should not. I then went on to say that, though I must await the orders of the Viceroy on the letter which the Amban had addressed him and could not, therefore, yet commence any formal negotiations, on the next occasion on which I should have the pleasure of meeting him and the Tibetan officials, I would state plainly and in detail the view which the Viceroy took of the situation, so that he and the Tibetans might know our views and be ready when the formal negotiations commenced to make proposals for their friendly settlement. To-day Mr. Ho and both Tibetan officials visited me, and after some ordinary conversation I said I now proposed to fulfill the promise I had made at our former meeting. While the interpreter was preparing to read the speech which I had had carefully translated into Tibetan by Captain O'Connor, the two Tibetan officials said they wished to raise objections to holding negotiations at Khamba Jong at all. The proper place for negotiation was, they said, at Giaogong. I told them that the place of meeting was a matter to be decided upon, not by the negotiators but by the Viceroy and Amban : and all the negotiators had to do was to carry on the negotiations in the place determined upon by their Excellencies. Much futile discussion upon this point followed, and then the two Tibetans raised objection to the size of my escort. I explained that it was merely the escort which was becoming to my rank and was even smaller than the escort which the Amban took to Darjeeling and Calcutta at the former negotiations. They said they had understood the negotiations were to be friendly, and so they themselves had brought no armed escort with them. I explained that the negotiations certainly were to be friendly : if I had had any hostile intentions, I would have brought many more than 200 men, who were only just sufficient to guard me against such attacks of bad characters as were very recently made upon the British Ambassador at the capital of the Chinese Empire. To put an end to these fruitless disputations, I motioned to the interpreter to commence reading my speech. Of this speech I have the honour to enclose a copy. It was not, of course, made for the benefit of these petty representatives here, but was intended to reach the ears of the Tibetan Government at Lhasa. Tibetan officials will receive no written communications from us : but I thought it barely possible they might pass on a verbal communication : and I had come to the conclusion that the Tibetan Government ought without delay to be in possession of a full statement of our position, as they are evidently under the impression that this is merely one other of the many fruitless frontier meetings which have taken place since the Convention was signed. The Tibetans listened attentively while the speech was being read : but at the conclusion the Grand Secretary said that he could not enter into any discussion about it. I said that I could not enter into any discussion either as I had received no orders yet from the Viceroy that he was satisfied that the Tibetan Government had sent representatives of sufficient rank and authority to meet me. I had, however, as a matter of courtesy, taken the trouble to acquaint them informally with the views the Viceroy held of the present position, and I trusted they would report what I had said to their

Government. They replied that they could not even do that much : that they could make no report at all unless we went back to the frontier at Giaogong, which was the place at which they meant to discuss matters. Mr. Ho, who had hitherto taken no part in the conversation, here said to me that these Tibetans were very ignorant and difficult to deal with, and he asked me if I could not meet them by agreeing to go to the frontier. I replied that I would with pleasure : and when representatives whom the Viceroy could permit me to enter into negotiations with were present, I would gladly ride with them to the frontier and discuss the question on the spot : but the frontier was not at Giaogong as the Tibetans supposed, but at the Serpubu La, only ten miles from here. Mr. Ho said that the actual position of the frontier was not known yet, but that it was where the waters flowed down towards India. I replied that five minutes' inspection would make clear where that was : and Mr. Ho said that then the matter would be very easily and quickly settled. Mr. Ho's Secretary then suggested that I should give the Tibetans the copy of my speech which the interpreter had just used. I assented with readiness, and with Mr. Ho's approval presented it to the Grand Secretary. But he could not have got rid of a viper with greater haste than he got rid of that paper. He said he could on no account receive it, and with the greatest concern he handed it to Mr. Ho's Secretary, to whom I had also given an English translation of my speech. But though these Tibetan officials professed their incapacity to report my speech to their Government I have not the smallest doubt they will. Messengers go from them every day to Lhasa, and it cannot be supposed that they would omit to mention in their letters so important event as to-day's interview. I expect, too, that, as Mr. Ho has the Tibetan text of my speech, he will send it on to the Amban, who in his turn will forward it to the Tibetan Government. I also hope to arrange through the Sikkim Maharaj Kumar that the Tibetan officials should have an opportunity of copying the Tibetan translation of my speech : and perhaps that copy may not be so repugnant to them as the original document The refusal of these two officials to receive, even with Mr. Ho's approval, merely the copy of a speech is, however, conclusive evidence they are quite unfit to eventually conduct negotiations with me. Mr Ho also acknowledges this, and Mr. White has from the first expressed the same opinion. They have no authority from their Government. Nor is Mr. Ho a man of much position or authority. He certainly has not the slightest influence over these Tibetans. On the other hand, he is very obstructive. In conclusion, I would add that both Mr. White and I are of the opinion that the Government of India must be prepared for very protracted negotiations : and also for the possible necessity for coercion before negotiations can be satisfactorily terminated. The attitude of the Tibetans is fully as obstructive and impracticable as Mr. White and every other person acquainted with them had predicted it would be : and I see at present little prospect of coming to a settlement without coercion. I however, use every possible means of argument and persuasion, and sincerely hope that the unfavorable opinion of the Tibetans I have formed from to-day's interview may be subsequently removed.

Annexure.

Copy of a speech made by Colonel F. E. Younghusband, C.I.E., at Khamba Jong.

TO THE TIBETAN REPRESENTATIVES—

I wish to take this opportunity of informing you that Mr. White and I have been sent by His Excellency the Viceroy of India to inquire into and settle certain frontier trade questions which have been the subject of correspondence between the British Chinese Governments. But, before entering into any formal discussion of these questions. I wish to state clearly to you, in an informal manner, the light in which we regard the matter so that, when I receive the orders of His Excellency to formally commence negotiations the representatives of the Chinese and Tibetan Governments, with whom I shall negotiate will not be unprepared with proposals for effecting a settlement.

You will remember, then, that 17 years ago, in the year 1886, the Viceroy proposed to send a peaceful Mission to Lhasa in accordance with a Treaty which the British Government had made with the Chinese Government 10 years before. British subjects had the right to trade in other parts and provinces of the Chinese Empire, just as all subjects of the Chinese

Emperor were allowed to trade, without any let or hindrance, in every part of the British Empire. But in this one single dependency of the Chinese Empire, insurmountable obstacles were always raised in the way of traders. It was to discuss this matter with Tibetan authorities at Lhasa, and to see if these obstacles to trade and intercourse between India and Tibet could not be removed that the then Viceroy of India proposed, with consent of the Chinese Government, to send a Mission to Lhasa in 1886.

But when the Mission was fully prepared to start, the Chinese Government, at that moment, informed the Viceroy that the Tibetans were so opposed to the idea of admitting a British Mission to their country that they (the Chinese Government) begged that Mission might be postponed. As an act of courtesy and out of good feeling towards Chinese Government, the Viceroy consented to their request and counter-ordered the Mission : but on the distinct understanding, laid down definitely in a Treaty between British and Chinese Governments signed in the same year, that the Chinese would "adopt measures to exhort and encourage the people with a view to the promotion and development of trade."

Seventeen years have passed away since this solemn promise was made by the Chinese Government, and, as I will show later on, the British Government have just cause to complain that in all those years, owing to your persistent obstruction, the Chinese Government have been unable to perform their pledge.

I have said that, out of deference to the wishes of the Chinese Government, the Viceroy consented to counter-order the Mission which he had intended to send to Lhasa. But this forbearance on the part of His Excellency met with a bad return on your part. You proceeded without any cause or justification to invade a State under British protection, and you even attacked British troops which had been sent there to protect it. The Viceroy bore this with patience for nearly two years, trusting that you would be obedient to the authority of the Chinese Government. But when you still remained in Sikkim, and still attacked the British troops there, he was compelled to punish you, to drive you from Sikkim, and to pursue you into Chumbi. And in Chumbi the British troops would have remained as a punishment for your unprovoked attack upon them if it had not been for the friendship which existed between your Suzerain, the Emperor of China, and the Queen of England.

But, out of regard for that friendship, the Viceroy agreed to enter into negotiations with the Amban at Lhasa acting on your behalf, and after some years, a Convention was concluded by which the boundary between Tibet and Sikkim was laid down; and arrangements were made for traders to be allowed to come to Yatung to sell their goods to whomsoever they pleased, to purchase native commodities, to hire transport, and to conduct their business without any vexatious restrictions. It was also agreed that, if after five years either side should wish to make any alterations, both parties should meet again and make a new agreement.

This was the Treaty which was signed by the Chinese Amban at Lhasa as representing the Chinese Emperor, and by the Viceroy of India as representing the Empress of India and Queen of Great Britain.

At the end of five years the Empress's Great Secretary of State wrote to the Viceroy of India and inquired how the Treaty was being observed by you. The Viceroy inquired of the Governor of Bengal, the Governor inquired of the Commissioner of Darjeeling. and the Commissioner of Darjeeling referred to Mr. White, the Political officer in Sikkim : and the report went back to the Great Secretary of State to the Empress that you had destroyed the boundary pillars which the British and Chinese officials had erected : that you had occupied land at Giaogong inside the line laid down by the Treaty : that you had built a wall on the other side of Yatung and allowed no one to pass through the gate to trade with the traders who came there from India : and, lastly, that you had repudiated the Treaty which had been signed by the Amban and the Viceroy of India because, you said, it had not been signed by one of yourselves.

Now, when the Empress's Great Secretary of State and His Excellency the Viceroy of India heard of the way you had set at nought the Treaty which had been signed by the representative of the Empress and the representative of the Emperor of China in your behalf, they were exceedingly angry, and the Viceroy ordered Mr. White to go to Giaogong and remove the

Tibetans who had presumed to come across the frontier which had been laid down in the Treaty which the Amban and the Viceroy had signed.

As you know, last year Mr. White went to Giaogong: he removed the Tibetans from from there, and threw down the guard-house, and reported to the Viceroy that he had carried out his Excellency's orders.

The Amban, hearing of these proceedings, wrote to the Viceroy that, if there was any matter for discussion about the frontier, he would send a Chinese officer and a representative of the Dalai Lama to settle it. And the Viceroy has now written, in reply, that he has sent a high officer to Khamba Jong and Mr. White with him to settle everything about the frontier and about trade. But as the Tibetans had broken the old Treaty because they said they had not known anything about it, his Excellency wrote to the Amban that, this time there must be present at the negotiations a Tibetan official of the highest rank whose authority to bind his Government must be unquestioned. Mr. White and I have come, then, by the orders of the Government of India to settle these matters, and as soon as I hear from the Viceroy that he is satisfied that this last request of his has been complied with, I shall be ready to commence the formal negotiations.

I can assure you that His Excellency has no intention whatever of permanently annexing your country, and it is possible he may, indeed, make concessions to you in regard to the lands near Giaogong

if in the coming negotiations you show yourselves
reasonable in regard to trade, and ready to put it on a
proper footing. His Excellency desires nothing better
than that you and we should live on good terms with
each other. This much I can tell you with confidence.
But I must also warn you that, after the way in which
you have broken and repudiated the old Treaty concluded in your interests by the Chinese Amban at the
close of a war in which you were heavily defeated,
you must expect that he will demand from you some
assurance that you will faithfully observe any new
settlement which we may arrive at.

You come and travel and trade in India just as
you please. You go where you like and stay there as
long as you like : and you are afforded protection
wherever you go. You yourself, Mr. Grand Secretary,
have enjoyed these privileges of British rule. But if
any one from India wishes to trade in Tibet, he is
stopped at once at the frontier, and no one is allowed
to go near him. He can trade in Russia, in Germany,
in France, and in all other great countries; and in all
other dependencies of the Chinese Empire except
Tibet-in Manchuria, in Mongolia, and in Turkistan.
But in Tibet alone of all countries he cannot trade.
This is a one-sided arrangement unworthy of so fair-
minded and cultured a people as you are; and
though, as I said before, His Excellency has no intention of annexing your country, and may indeed, if
you prove reasonable in regard to the admission of
trade, make concessions to you in respect to the
frontier lands near Giaogong, yet he will insist that

the obstacles you have for so many years put in the way of trade between India and Tibet shall be once and for ever removed.

I have told you plainly what Mr. White and I have come here to do; and I wish you to explain to your Government fully and carefully the words I have spoken: and when they have fully considered these words, I hope they will send wise and experienced and trusted Councillors to assist the representative of the Chinese Government, and make proposals to Mr. White and me as to the way in which we can best establish those friendly relations and means of communication which ought to subsist between two neighbouring and friendly countries.

∞◦◆◦∞

Diary kept by Captain W. F. O'Connor during the Tibet Frontier Mission, 1903.
(Extract.)

9th July, 1903.—Rain fell during the night and continued in a light drizzle till about 9 a.m.

Mr. Ho passed our camp about 9.30 coming from Giri to Khamba Jong. I received him on the road (guard presented arms) before the camp, enquired after his health, and requested him to call on Mr.

White with the Tibetan officers on the following day. We shifted our camp to a better site, some 100 yards or so further from the hill. The Tibetan officers who were expected at Khamba Jong to-day did not arrive. The Maharaj Kumar of Sikkim rode into camp in the evening after a long cold ride from Tangu.

10th July.—The sky still overcast by heavy clouds. The monsoon seems to have reached this district, and light rain falls at intervals.

The two Lhasa officials passed our camp at 11 a.m. I received them on the road with the same ceremony as in the case of Ho, presenting Mr. White's compliments, and requesting them to call upon him on the following day when they were recovered from the fatigues of their journey, to which they agreed. The Jougpen visited the camp during the day with presents for Mr. White and the Kumar Sikkim. I had a long conversation with him in my tent. He was very friendly and communicative. Major Bretherton, who was to have left to-day for Tangu, was detained by an attack of ague.

Meteorological observations established to-day, but the instruments are not at all satisfactory.

11th July.—A fine morning, but the air full of aqueous vapour, and the temperature perceptibly cooler than on the first two days of our stay here. Minimum temperature last night 39°.

The two Tibetan officers-the Depon and the Tung-yig-Chembo-called at 11 a.m., accompanied by a small escort of 8 or 10 mounted men and some retainers. They were received at the entrance to camp and conducted to the Durbar tent, where Mr. White received and greeted them. The Tung-yig-Chembo, as an ecclesiastic, is the senior of the two. He is a man of 45 years of age, intelligent, and very voluble, with a shrewd and a rather complacent cast of countenance. The Depon appears to be a man some years younger, and with a face devoid of much character. Both are well-mannered, but have a slightly uneasy appearance, and no air of authority. The conversation was chiefly confined to trivialities, and some protests from the officials regarding our transgression of the boundary. They would appear to be in ignorance of the Viceroy's letter to the Amban, and of the reply of the latter thereto; or, if they are acquainted with them, they wilfully ignore their import. After leaving Mr. White, they visited the Kumar in his tent, where I also conversed with them for some time. I was especially anxious to secure from them some expression to indicate that they were acting in this matter under direct orders from their own Government uninfluenced by the Chinese. But they evaded all queries, and merely reiterated that, if they had not had proper orders, they would not, of course, be here. Later, when the subject of Mr. White's return visit was mooted, they objected entirely to his visiting at the Jong, and suggested having a tent prepared for his reception at the foot of the hill. As they were at the time residing at the Jong, and as the Jong is the official head-quarters of the district, it seemed to Mr. White that such a reception would not be at all suitable, and after requesting the officials to reconsider the matter, the return call upon them was postponed until the following day.

At 1 p.m. Mr. White, accompanied by a small escort, left camp to call upon Mr. Ho. On arrival at Mr. Ho's camp, it was found that the two Lhasa officers were also present, and Mr. White sent a message to Mr. Ho, requesting him to receive him (Mr. White) alone. The Tibetans accordingly withdrew, and a short visit was paid to Mr. Ho. Mr. Ho was somewhat perturbed regarding the proposed visit to the Jong, and, whilst quite recognising that this was the proper place for Mr. White to be received, he was inclined to defer to the wishes of the Tibetans in the matter. As an instance of the curious position held by the Chinese in this country, it is worth noting that whilst the Tibetans defer to Mr. Ho in almost every matter, going even so far as to forward to him official letters received from our camp for fear that they may get into trouble if they retained them themselves, Mr. Ho himself admitted that in many matters he was powerless, and that had we not already crossed the boundary, it was certain that Mr. Parr, who has been nominated by the Amban as a Chinese Commissioner, would not have been allowed to cross, and that even now he would not be admitted beyond the wall at Yatung, should he desire to proceed to Khamba Jong via the Chumbi valley. The Tibetan officials, in fact, appear to be childishly impotent and terrified of their own Government, whilst at the same time they are deliberately obstructive in every matter, great or small, in which the British are concerned, and are quite ready to use the Chinese as a very convenient scape-goat whenever it suits them to do so.

The Kumar visited the Jong in the evening, and was received there by the Tibetans, who begged him to use his influence to dissuade Mr. White from visiting the Jong the following day.

12th July.—A fine morning, but the sky all overcast by heavy clouds drifting north-east. Minimum temperature last night 39.8°; maximum yesterday 60°.

The difficulty regarding the return call upon the two Tibetans was arranged as follows. Mr. White sent word to the Jong that, if the officials would receive me at the entrance to the Jong in order to discuss the situation, it was possible he might waive his just claim to be received in the Jong itself; and Mr. White instructed me to endeavour to induce the two Tibetans to produce their written orders from Lhasa in return for this concession on his part. I accordingly rode up to the Jong about 11 a.m., accompanied by the Kumar of Sikkim, and we were received by the two officials at the entrance. A long and very interesting conversation, lasting more than two hours, then followed. We began by generalities and elicited the fact that the Tung-yig-Chembo is a great traveller-has been to Pekin and back viâ Calcutta and Shanghai. But on approaching official subjects, a deadlock ensued at once. The Tibetans' argument is somewhat as follows: "The proper place appointed by our Government for the discussion of affairs is the

Giaogong frontier. On arrival there we will produce our credentials." From this position it was impossible to move them, except so far that they would consent, although it was irregular, to show the letter to the Kumar. With this it was necessary to be satisfied, but in the long desultory conversation which we had, several interesting facts came to light. The officials for one thing plainly expressed their dislike for the Chinese, who, they said, despised the Tibetans and were often instrumental in admitting foreigners into the country. As regards official correspondence, they said that, by the terms of some treaty between the Chinese and Tibetans, all official correspondence between the Tibetans and foreigners had to be conducted through the Ambans. Under the circumstances, they could neither receive nor reply to our letters. But they affirmed, nevertheless, that they were fully empowered to treat with our Commissioners at the proper place-the Giaogong frontier.

It has been arranged that Mr. White shall pay his return call upon the Tibetans to-morrow, and they and Mr. Ho have been asked to luncheon at our camp afterwards.

A letter was written to-day to Mr. Ho, requesting him to use his influence with the Tibetans to induce them to provide us daily with a certain quantity of grass or chopped straw as fodder for our animals.

13th July, 1903.—Fine bright morning. Light varying breeze. Maximum temperature 65.6°; minimum 35.9°.

About noon Mr. White, accompanied by a small escort, left camp and rode through the village of Khamba to call upon the two Tibetan officers in the tents which they had pitched near the foot of the hill upon which the Jong is built. A short interview ensued, during which no subjects of importance were broached, and the conversation was confined to generalities and to some remarks from the Tung-yig-Chembo regarding his travels to China. Both of the officers complained of ill-health which they attributed to the water. At the close of the interview Mr. White presented some presents to the two officials and to the Jongpen, each present including two packets of Indian tea. The Jongpen tried to raise some objection to receiving the tea, but no attention was paid to him, and the presents were accepted.

In the evening Mr. White took some photographs of the Jong, and he and I rode some distance up the nulla behind the Jong.

We decided to ride out to Dobta, on a place to the north of the Tsomo-tel-tung lake, about twenty miles distant, on the following day, to encamp there for a day or two, and to return via Tinki Jung. Dobta is a kind of fief of the Maharaja of Sikkim, whence he draws an annual supply of grain and other local produce. Mr. White decided that the Kumar of Sikkim, who was anxious to visit Dobta and the neighbourhood, should accompany our party.

14th July.—Fine bright morning. Sky clear of clouds,

only a low belt on the horizon. Maximum temperature 66.5°: minimum 35°.

We packed up all our kit and loaded it upon yaks,
and started the baggage off for Dobta about 9 A.M.
Just as we had finished breakfast ourselves, word was
brought that Mr. Ho, accompanied by the two
Tibetan officers, was approaching our camp.
Conjecturing that this foreboded an energetic protest
against our proposed expedition, Mr. White asked me
to receive the officials and to hear what they had to
say. I conducted them to my tent where a long
discussion ensued lasting over two hours. Mr Ho
began by protesting against our proposed move, saying that the orders from our Government authorised
us to come as far as Khamba Jong, but gave us no
authority to proceed further, or to any other place in
Tibet. To which I replied that we had no orders to
forbid to proceed further afield, and that it was unrea-
sonable to expect that we should remain cooped up
in the limits of a small camp. Obviously no satisfactory conclusion could come from such arguments as
these, and I begged the Tibetans to show us any written authority from their Government, instructing
them to hinder our movements, or which authorized
them in any way to interfere with travellers in their
country. They replied that they had no such orders,
but that what they told us was the custom of their
country. Meanwhile we learnt that there was a considerable gathering of unarmed men in and about the
Jong, and that our yaks and servants had been actually
stopped and turned back a mile or so from camp. So

in view of the energetic protests of the three officials, and in order to avoid any possibility of a fracas, Mr. White consented to defer his visit to Dobta, pending reference to the Indian Government, on receipt from the Tibetan officers of a written request informing him that it was not the custom in Tibet to allow travellers or any other foreigners to move about the country, and begging him to defer his visit to Dobta. When these terms were made known, the two Tibetans became very excited and voluble. They explained again that it was impossible for them either to give or receive written communications, but that all letters must pass through Mr. Ho. All the old arguments had to be gone through over again. I pointed out to them that, as representatives of the Lhasa Government, they were surely entitled, after consultation with Mr. Ho if they so desired, to communicate directly with Mr. White on a matter which concerned customs and laws purely Tibetan. I explained to them that, in the matter of the Sikkim Frontier Convention, which was signed by a Chinese plenipotentiary, the Tibetans had ever since disavowed the Treaty; and that consequently we were no longer prepared to accept the signature of any Chinaman, however high in rank, as a sufficient guarantee for binding the Tibetans in any matter, great or small. All these arguments were of no avail. Without attempting to reply to them, the Tibetans kept asserting that it was not their custom to write letters to foreigners, and that they refuse to begin now. After a long period of futile discussion, Mr. White sent in word that he proposed to start in half an hour if his terms were not complied with. This brought matters to a crisis, and I suggested, as a solution of the difficulty which we were all anxious to settle amicably, that Mr. Ho should write and sign a letter in Chinese and the Tibetans in Tibetan, having the purport required by Mr. White. Mr. Ho, who behaved most sensibly throughout the interview, at once agreed, and urged upon the two Tibetans to do the same. These latter, much perturbed, went outside to consult whilst pens and paper were produced, and I drafted a letter in English which was at once translated into Chinese and Tibetan. Mr. Ho signed his letter without demur, glad to be rid so easily of so petty and annoying an incident. But the two Tibetans were troublesome in the extreme. At first they objected to the terms of the letter which was brief and unobjectionable to a degree. They then found fault with the title by which they were described, which was a common Tibetan word meaning Commissioner. When this had been put right, and they saw that signature was inevitable, I suddenly saw the Jongpen making his way to the table pen in hand. Asking the meaning of this I was told that, as neither of the Tibetan officers could write (they are both, I believe, very well educated men), they proposed that the Jongpen should sign for them. I objected to this altogether, and Mr. Ho was so enraged at their obstinacy and folly that, after shrieking at them for some moments in Chinese, he rushed out of the tent, declaring he was going home. He was, however, soothed and brought back, but even then the Tibetan representatives continued their absurd behaviour. The Tung-yig-Chembo, with a pen in his hand, kept making darts at the upper end of the letter, hoping to conceal his signature amongst the rest of the writing; but being frustrated in this, and firmly shown where his signature was expected, he succeeded in making a perfectly meaningless mark at the very end of the letter. Whilst I was expostulating with him on the folly of this proceeding, the Depon seized the opportunity to make another mark, more complicated in appearance, but equally devoid of significance, alongside that of the Tung-yig. It was impossible to accept these marks as signatures, and at length, when orders had been given that Mr. White would march in five minutes, the Tung-yig wrote a couple of words, purporting to be the signatures of himself and the Depon at the foot of the letter. With this we were obliged to be satisfied, and the Maharaj Kumar of Sikkim and myself witnessed the signature. In reply to the letter, Mr. White gave a written communication to each party to say that he had considered their letters, and that in deference to their wishes, he would postpone his visit to Dobta, pending reference to his own Government. Mr. Ho took his answer, but the Tung-yig-Chembo was about to refuse to accept his when I slipped it into his hand, and he handed it instantly across the table to Mr. Ho. The three officials then took their departure.

It may appear that a great deal of space has been devoted to so trivial an incident; but the details have been given in full as typical of the non possumus attitude adopted by the Tibetan representatives. "We cannot accept letters; we cannot write letters; we cannot let you into our zone; we cannot let you travel; we cannot discuss matters because this is not the proper place; go back to Giaogong and send away all your soldiers, and we will come to an agreement." It is easy to see what such an agreement would amount to. Their last words, as they left camp, were to ask us not to make a walk round our camp, as it was not in accordance with the custom of the country.

There was a fairly large gathering of men at the Jong this morning, evidently brought together with the idea of preventing us from going to Dobta; but they were all unarmed (though there are said to be arms in the Jong), and there is little doubt that, had we persisted in our intention of starting, we could have made our way through them with little more trouble than we had at Giaogong.

15th July.—A fine morning. Scattered cumulus clouds and a light south-east breeze. Maximum temperature 70.9°; minimum 36.5°.

A message was sent to Mr. Ho by Mr. White, informing him that Captain Parr was unwell, and asking him whether he would allow a full translation into English to be made of the Amban's dispatch to the Viceroy, in order to save further loss of time in forwarding this document. Mr. Ho replied that the original despatch had been already forwarded to Captain Parr. Mr. Ho and the Tibetan officers still complain of ill-health. There is no further news today.

I give the following rumours derived from native information for what they are worth. That the Tale Lama does not now intend to come to Shigatse. That 200 soldiers under eight Dingpons are coming to Taktakang Gompa, some 20 miles from here, from Shigatse. That Mr. Parr will not be allowed by the Tibetans to come here via Chumbi, as it is believed he proposes to do. That Mr. Ho, presumably after his experience of the Tibetan officials yesterday, proposes to write to the Amban with a view of having more influential representatives sent.

16th July, 1903.—A fine bright morning. Maximum temperature yesterday 67.9°; minimum temperature last night 35°.

Mr. White, the Maharaj Kumar of Sikkim, and I started off at 8 a.m., and rode off in a west-south-west direction following a well marked track till we reached the banks of the Yarn Chu, near the village of Tak-nag. Our route led us over the level plain which I have previously described, and which appears to be reserved by the people for the winter grazing of their sheep and goats. Opposite Tak-nag village the stream is spanned by a rough timber bridge supported on small stone piers two or three feet high. Total length of bridge 40 paces, roadway some two or three feet wide and sodded. Tak-nag is a little village of three or four houses surrounded by a good stretch of barley cultivation and some fields of radishes. Passing to the village we rode up the opposite hill to the Pari Gompa, which is perched on top of the hill. The lower slopes of the hill

are barren, but after rising two or three hundred feet
we found the whole hillside well covered with juniper
and other bushes. The higher we got the stronger the
vegetation became, and we were surprised to find near
the top of the hill, at an elevation which cannot be less
than 16,000 feet, big bushes of juniper with trunks and
branches as thick as a man's arm. Apart from the
wormwood scrub which we are now burning in camp,
and of which there is an unlimited supply within easy
reach, this one hillside alone would afford fuel for an
army for many months. Half-way up the hill we passed
the little hamlet of Gousa–no cultivation, but plenty of
excellent grazing. The monastery at the top of the hill
is a dirty, tumble-down group of buildings inhabited
by a few so-called hermits and some nuns. They get
their water from a little spring at Gousa. Riding westwards along the top of the hill, we had an excellent
view of the Tsomo-tel-tung lake and of the great plain
in which it lies. The lake lies in the westward end of the
plain very much as represented in Mr. White's map of
the Sikkim-Tibet frontier region. It is a wide sheet of
blue water enclosed on three sides by hills with two
steep-sided promontories projecting into it from the
north. It was all visible except the extreme south-west
corner. The question of its drainage is still unsolved.
But this matter will be further investigated, and I propose to report at fuller length upon this and other
geographical questions when I am better acquainted
with the country. In the plain directly north of us we
could see with our glasses numerous large flocks of
sheep and some yaks feeding in the grassy stretches.

The sheep must have numbered many thousands. No survey was attempted, as, owing to mist on the surrounding hill tops it was impossible to fix our position accurately. In the plain to our north and round about the lake, some 15 villages or more were visible. We returned past the Gompa and down the hill by a slightly different route, shooting 10 hares on the way and a brace of hill-partridges–one of which we cannot yet identify. Reaching the plain, we crossed the Chi-Chn and the Yam-Chu–the former some 50 feet in breadth, the latter only 10 or 12, and passed the village of Tagha–three or four houses and some very good barley fields, and reached camp at Khamba Jong at 6 p.m. The villagers we met during the day were quite friendly and ready to enter into conversation. Black rain clouds brooded all day over the mountain range to the north, and there appeared to be heavy rain on them and in the Tsangpo valley.

17th July.—Rain fell here during the night. A cloudy morning. Maximum temperature yesterday 69°; minimum last night, 39°.

Day in camp. A showery evening. The Jongpen, in return for a very liberal rate of payment, is supplying us with some grass and chopped straw.

18th July.—A wet night, rain continuing till about 6.30 a.m. Maximum temperature, 66.6°; minimum, 39.6°.

Mr. Ho's Munshi came into camp at 11 a.m., and was informed that Colonel Younghusband was expected at 5 p.m. He said that Mr. Ho was unwell, and would be unable personally to meet Colonel Younghusband, but that he would send his Deputy and would inform the two Tibetan officers of the British Commissioner's arrival. Captain Bethune and I rode as far as Giri, where we met Colonel Younghusband and rode with him back to camp. Colonel Younghusband had ridden straight from Tangu, and was accompanied by Mr. Dover and a few mounted men. Just before reaching camp he was met by Mr. Ho's English-speaking Chinese Deputy and by the Jongpen of Khamba Jong. Mr. Ho's Deputy brought Mr. Ho's compliments and greetings to the Commissioner, and the Jongpen presented a scarf on behalf of the two Tibetan officials, neither of whom appeared in person. The approach to the camp was lined by the men of the escort who saluted as the Commissioner rode through.

19th July.—Cloudy morning. Maximum temperature yesterday 62.8°; minimum temperature last night 44°. The warmest night we have had as yet. Heavy shower about 12.30 a.m.

At 1 p.m. the Jongpen called upon the Commissioner accompanied by two officers in the suite of the Tung-yig-Chembo and the Depon, and bringing some presents. They were received by Colonel Younghusband, who conversed with them for some time, and sent friendly messages to the two Tibetan officials. Later, Mr. Ho's Deputy also called, bringing presents from Mr. Ho, and was received by

Colonel Younghusband, who has arranged to call upon Mr. Ho, at 4 p.m. to-morrow. During the afternoon Mr. White and I rode across the Khamba Jong plain to a small hill some three or four miles distant in a westerly direction, where we found a few fossils amongst the debris on the hillside.

The two Tibetan officers are still residing in the Jong which they have now completely closed, not only to ourselves, but to all servants and followers from our camp.

20th July, 1903.—A fine morning with a light southerly breeze and a few scattered clouds. Maximum temperature 75.8°; minimum 38.5°.

The Khamba Jongpen came into camp about noon whilst Mr. Bailey and the Kumar were playing with the gramophone. He was greatly tickled with the instrument, and could not refrain from roars of laughter at anything which struck him as particularly funny. He was accompanied by the former Jongpen, who, it appears, has been sent here from Tashi Chunpo (where he acts, so he told me, as a sort of headmen to the Penchen Rinpochi) to assist the present incumbent of the office at this difficult juncture. I saw them both in my tent where we discussed the following matters:-The question of some damage done to two Chortens (a sort of religious edifice) near the camp; compensation to be paid by us for the grazing land round the Jong and for the fuel we burn; the matter of the hut now being built half-way between here and Tangu. These were all trivial matters, and will probably be arranged to the satisfaction of both parties. The question of the fuel was only raised, I think, to see whether anything could be extracted from us by way of compensation. All fuel used in camp consists of small wormwood bushes which grow on the surrounding hills and plains in absolutely unlimited quantities and can have no market value. The Jongpen was asked to inform the two Tibetan officers that the British Commissioners proposed to call upon Mr. Ho that day at 4 p.m., and that they would be pleased to see the two officials at the same hour at the Chinese camp at 4 p.m. Colonel Younghusband, Mr. White, Captain Bethune, and myself rode down to Mr. Ho's camp in full dress preceded by 50 men of the escort. The Commissioners were received by Mr. Ho and by the Tung-yig-Chembo, the Depon being too unwell to attend. The visit was a short one and no question of interest was raised, Mr. Ho merely remarking that Khamba Jong was not a healthy spot, and that he and the two Tibetan officers had all been indisposed since arrival here. On returning to camp presents were sent to Mr. Ho by the hand of Mr. Mitter, Colonel Younghusband's head clerk. Mr. Mitter on his return reported that he had found the Tung-yig-Chembo still in Mr. Ho's camp and evidently expecting a present also. Presents were, therefore, prepared for the Tung-yig-Chembo, the Depon, and the Jongpen, and despatched with Mr. Mitter to the Jong. Mr. Mitter was not admitted to the Jong, but the Tung-yig-Chembo descended to the entrance and the presents were accepted and appeared to cause pleasure.

21st July.—A lovely bright morning. Maximum temperature yesterday 67.5°; minimum 38.9°.

Mr. White and I starting at 5.30 a.m. rode up the Khamba Jong nulla to the pass at the head-some six to seven miles. From a hill at the head of the nulla (elevation 18,500 feet) we had a good view of the country to the north and east. This piece of country is drained by the upper waters of the Yarn Chu, whose feeders flow in level, open valleys, well grassed in places, with "doks," or headmen's encampments, here and there, but no houses. The hills bounding the basin of the Yam Chu are uniformly low and easy in outline, and their passage at any point should present no difficulties. Two roads appear to lead to Gyangtse from near the point we were on. One running almost due east must join the Chumbi trade route near the Kalo Tso; the other going north-east runs direct to Gyangtse, and judging from the appearance of the country can present no great obstacles to movement. But we could discern no sign of the bushes which are so useful as fuel round about Khamba Jong. It is probable that, should we have to move later to Gyangtse, we should have to carry with us all fuel and supplies. There should be plenty of grazing (from now on till the autumn) for yaks and country ponies. We returned along the crest of the ridge bounding the north side of the nulla in hope of finding some game, but saw nothing except herds of female burrhel. We reached camp at 2 p.m.

22nd July.—A still cloudy morning. Maximum temperature 70.9°; minimum 43.5°.

At 2 p.m. Mr. Ho and the two Tibetan officers called on the British Commissioners, and were received with due honours. The interview which followed lasted an hour and a-half. Colonel Younghusband began by explaining that, pending receipt of orders from the Viceroy, no formal discussion was possible, but that he proposed to explain to the Chinese and Tibetan representatives the views which the Government of India took regarding the progress of events which had led to the necessity for negotiations. In the conversation which followed, the two Tibetan officials took a leading part and expatiated at length on their two principal grievances-the fact of our having crossed the frontier and of having brought an armed escort into the country. They reiterated their claim to have Giaogong regarded as the place of meeting, and urged various arguments in support of their views; and thus protested against the introduction into Tibet of the escort as incompatible with the intentions of a peaceful mission and as likely to raise suspicions in the minds of the Tibetans. It was in vain that Colonel Younghusband explained to them that it was the custom of our country to attach an escort to officers of high rank, and that its presence by no means indicated hostile intentions; and that, as regards the boundary, the question was one to be settled later, and that meanwhile we claim up to the watershed of the Teesta. They kept repeating their requests and urging their consideration. Mr. Ho contented himself with remarking that he thought it would be well to ascertain exactly where the watershed of the Teesta lay, and Colonel Younghusband professed himself perfectly ready to do so as soon as the negotiations began in earnest. Colonel Younghusband's speech was then read aloud in Tibetan. In this Colonel Younghusband explained that no formal negotiations could take place until the receipt of further orders from the Viceroy, and that meanwhile he took these means of making the Chinese and Tibetan representatives acquainted with the views of the Viceroy and of the course of events on the Sikkim-Tibet frontier during the last seventeen years. Then followed a résume of these events dating from the time of the proposed Macaulay Mission, and detailing all important matters up to the present time. And the speech concluded by pointing out the one-sided nature of the existing relations between Tibet and India as regards matters of trade, and with the hope that the Lhasa Government would consider the matter carefully, and would send experienced and trusted councillors to assist in bringing about friendly and satisfactory relations between the two countries. The two Tibetans listened attentively to the speech, and at its conclusion the Tung-yig-Chembo remarked that, whilst not proposing how to enter into discussion regarding what he had heard, he must observe that previous to the Convention of 1890 the trade with India via the

Chumbi valley was of insignificant proportions and in the hands of petty traders; but that since that time it had increased very materially and was now conducted by wealthy merchants. His point seemed to be that, as the trade was in so satisfactory a condition, he did not well understand what more we wanted. An English copy of the speech was given to Mr. Ho, and a Tibetan copy to the Tung-yig-Chembo, who, however, at once handed it over to Mr. Ho's interpreter. The interview concluded shortly afterwards and the officials took their leave.

∞∞◈∞∞

23rd July, 1903.—Fine still morning. Some light clouds in the sky. Maximum temperature yesterday 67.8°; minimum last night 41°.

Colonel Younghusband and Mr. White rode out during the day to visit the Kozo hot spring, which lies in a valley some two or three miles north of Khamba Jong. They found the temperature of the hottest spring to be 175°F. A young Tibetan from the Chinese camp visited me in the evening, and I had an interesting conversation with him regarding Tibetan manners and customs. His elder brother is a monk in Sera monastery, and he tells me the monks of the three big monasteries are a truculent lot-regularly drilled, bitterly hostile to foreigners, and apparently spoiling for a fight. Arms of sorts for all the monks are stored in the monasteries. He tells me that the nominal number of monks in Sera - 5,500 - is far below the reality, and similarly in De-bung and Ga-den. He is the third brother of four, and the three younger have one wife between them. He explained a good many of the household arrangements, and I hope to get hold of him again and learn some more. He says Mr. Ho detests this place. The water doesn't agree with him, and he has a bucket (of the Tibetan pattern) of water brought to him daily from Giaogong, at a cost of 12 annas. Like all the poorer class of Tibetans he complains of the extortions of the officials in the matter of taxes and forced carriage (kar begar of the North-West). He says every penny we pay here for grass and so on goes into the pockets of the Jongpen, and nothing whatever reaches the wretched misser, or peasant.

24th July.—Fine morning. Light southerly breeze. Maximum temperature yesterday 67.8°; minimum 36.5°.

I spent the morning in camp collecting information regarding the Tibetan Government and the Tsong-du-Chembo, or great national assembly, in which, as might be expected, the powerful Abbots of the three great monasteries have a preponderating influence. As usual, the information of my informants was most conflicting, and will have to be rigorously checked. The difficulty is to get hold of men of position and real knowledge. Servants and peasants naturally have very sketchy ideas on affairs of State. The Te-ling Kusho, the son of the old Pagh Diwan of Sikkim, called on the Sikkim Kumar to day and spent most of the day conversing in his tent. He is a stout pleasant-faced young man of 29, and has rank of Dung-Kor with no duties attached to it. He has two estates in Tibet, one at Te-ling just north of here, on the southern slopes of the central chain, and one near She-kar Jong (the Shikar Jong of the maps) in the Brahmaputra valley, where he tells me he gets good and enormous crops. He has frequently visited Lhasa, and gave me some interesting information. He is staying with the Jongpen in the Jong.

25th July.—Cloudy morning. Maximum temperature 71°; minimum 39.5°.

I sent off two men to Taktsang Gompa to see if they could meet the Tibetan soldiers and bring us back word how they were armed, &c. The Te-ling Kusho came again and spent most of the day with the Kumar. Like most unofficial Tibetans I have met, he appears to entertain a cordial dislike to his own Government and its methods. He told Mr. White that he and most men in his position would be only too delighted to see the country opened up to trade, and there can be no doubt that this is the case. All enterprise and enlightenment in this country is stifled by the great monk faction, who are well aware that progress is fatal to their influence. In the course of my enquiries one very strong exposition, on which the Chinese take their stand in Tibetan politics, has been frequently emphasised. This position is due to the fact that the three Lhasa monasteries-Sera, De-bung, and Ga-den-are directly subsidised by the Chinese Emperor. The subsidy takes the form chiefly, according to the popular idea generally prevalent, of a daily free tea to all the monks of these monasteries. The consequence is that the Lama faction, by far the strongest in Tibetan politics, is an uncompromising supporter of China. Any policy likely to be distasteful to China is vigorously opposed by the monks, for fear that by offending China they may lose their Chinese grant. I have frequently heard this argument used as one of the reasons why the Tibetans so persistently oppose the introduction into Tibet of Indian tea. It is thought that should the Chinese tea trade decline, the grant to the "Sen-de-gye-sum" (the three great monasteries) would be withheld. And the same argument is applied in many other matters where Chinese and Tibetan interests conflict. Of this I can give various examples. But it may be asked how the monastic influence is brought to bear on a Government in which three out of the four principal Ministers (Shapes) are laymen. The fact seems to be that lying behind the Tale Lama, the Shapes, and all the machinery of the Tibetan Government, as we have hitherto been acquainted with it, there is an institution called the "Tsong-du-chembo" or "Tsong-du gze-tsom," which may reasonably be compared with what we call a "National Assembly" or, as the word implies, "Great Assembly." It is constituted of the Kenpas or Abbots of the three great monasteries, representative from the four linqs or small monasteries actually in Lhasa city and from all the other monasteries in the province of U, and besides this all the officials of the Government are present–laymen and ecclesiastics alike–to the number of several hundreds. It is said, but I do not yet know with what truth, that the Tale Lama presides in person. The Tsong-du then is the assemblage of all the notables of Central Tibet, and some of my informants tell me that the provinces-Tsong and Kam-are represented as well. No fixed time or period is laid down for the meeting of the assembly. It is convoked only upon occasions of national need or importance; but more especially with reference to frontier matters. In the Tsong-du meetings the Abbots of the three great monasteries appear to be the preponderating influence–held in consideration far above the Shapes or any other Government officials, and this is natural when we recollect that they are backed by a following of above 20,000 armed and bigoted monks within easy reach. Their views and that of their brother Abbots from elsewhere undoubtedly sway the assembly and dictate the policy of the country. There can be, in fact, no one to oppose them. The civil troops of Tibet are despicable and number no more than some 6,000 altogether.

Ho has requested the Jongpen to supply us, as far as he can, with what supplies we require as a standing order; and the Jongpen appears glad enough to make all the profit he can out of so favourable an opportunity.

Letter from Colonel F. E. Younghusband, C.I.E., British Commissioner, Tibet Frontier Commission, to the Secretary to the Government of India, in the Foreign Department, dated Khamba Jong, the 27th July, 1903.
(Extract.)

I have the honour to forward a despatch just received, dated the 24th June, 1903, with its translation in English, from the Chinese Resident at Lhasa, in reply to His Excellency the Viceroy's despatch of the 3rd idem.
Annexure

Yü, Chinese Imperial Resident at Lhasa, charged with the administration of Tibetan affairs, Brevet Lieutenant-General of the Manchu Brigade, &c., to His Excellency the Right Honourable Baron Curzon of Kedleston, P.C., G.M.S.I., G.M.I.E., &c., &c., Viceroy and Governor-General of India, dated Lhasa, Kuang Hsir 29th year, 5th Moon, and 29th day (24th June, 1903).
(Translation.)

YOUR EXCELLENCY,
I have the honour to acknowledge the receipt, on the 21st instant, of Your Excellency's despatch, dated the 3rd June, 1903, and understand its contents. We should now discuss and settle any matters. Last year in July I deputed Prefect Ho, Kuang-hsieh of the 3rd

rank and decorated with the Peacock's Feather, to proceed to frontier to discuss matters, and the Yatung Commissioner, Parr, decorated with the 3rd class of the Imperial Order of Double Dragon, as Joint Commissioner. But last year in September Mr. Ho had to return to Lhasa on account of illness, which it was impossible to foresee; therefore, he did not meet Your Excellency's Commissioner, which was truly unfortunate. When Mr. Ho had recovered, I instructed him quickly to return to Yatung, where he has now awaited Your Excellency's Deputy for over half a year. I was much pleased to receive Your Excellency's despatch, and learn that Your Excellency had deputed Colonel Young-husband, a Resident in Your Political Department, and the Political Officer in Sikkim, Mr. White, to meet at Khamba Jong on the 7th July to discuss matters. I sincerely wish both countries to discuss and settle any matters in a friendly spirit, and now still depute Mr. Ho, in conjunction with Mr. Commissioner Parr, to quickly proceed and discuss matters. Mr. Ho is a civil official of the 3rd rank, and Commissioner Parr holds the 3rd class of the Imperial Order of the Double Dragon, truly of equal rank to the Commissioners deputed by Your Excellency, so both sides should discuss all matters in a friendly manner. With regard to the Tibetan officials, I have communicated with the Dalai Lama, and he has deputed his Chief Secretary, Lo-Pu-Ts'ang Ch'Êng-lo, and Wang-ch'ü Chieh-Pu, Depon of Lhasa, and decorated with the Peacock's Feather, to proceed and negotiate in conjunction with the

Chinese Commissioners. But I understand that Khamba Jong is in Tibetan territory; therefore, the British Commissioners and the Chinese and Tibetan Commissioners deputed by me are only able to rendezvous at the boundary near the grazing grounds fixed by the Convention of 1890. Moreover, Your Excellency informs me that the 7th of July is the date fixed. When I received Your Excellency's despatch there were then only a little over 10 days for me to instruct Mr. Ho and Commissioner Parr to proceed to Khamba from Yatung, and also to depute the Tibetan officials and get ready our baggage. I fear, therefore, that it will be impossible for all to arrive up to time, but have notwithstanding urged my Commissioners to use despatch. I sincerely hope that some plan can be discussed by which frontier and trade relations can be settled, and thus the long-standing friendship existing between our countries, also the friendly relations existing with Tibet may continue. I therefore write this communication and beg Your Excellency's kind consideration.

A necessary despatch.

Letter from Colonel F. E. Younghusband, C.I.E., British Commissioner, Tibet Frontier Commission, to the Secretary to the Government of India, in the Foreign Department, dated Khamba Jong, the 29th July, 1903.
(Extract.)

I have the honour to report that last night Captain Parr informed me that a Deputy from the Tashi

Lama would call upon me to-day "to demand the reason of our armed presence within the country of his august master, and to request our immediate withdrawal." I would have been within my rights in refusing to receive him as he was not deputed by either the Chinese or the Lhasa authorities; but these Tibetans are so ignorant that I do not like to lose any opportunity. I therefore consented to receive him. The Deputy said he had been sent by the Tashi Lama to represent to us that he was put to great trouble with the Lhasa authorities by our presence here; that the Lhasa authorities held him responsible for permitting us to cross the frontier; and he begged that I would kindly save him from this trouble by withdrawing across the frontier or to Yatung, which was the place fixed for meetings of this kind. I explained to him and his associates very carefully that Mr. White and I had been sent to discuss certain frontier and trade matters with delegates who would be appointed by the Chinese and Tibetan Governments, and that the place where these nego-tiations should be carried on was a matter for decision by my Government in consultation with the Chinese Government. In this matter of the meeting place for negotiations I had absolutely no discretion. They then said that they would petition the Chinese : and I told them the Amban had already represented the matter to his Government : and that all we officials on the spot could do was to abide by the decision which our Governments had come to. I then explained to them, for the benefit of their master, the reason of our presence here : how they had without provocation attacked our troops in Sikkim : how we had defeated them : how the Amban had come and interceded for them : how we had concluded a Treaty arranging for trade at Yatung and fixing the boundary of Sikkim at the water-parting between the Teesta River and the rivers of Tibet : how they had prevented traders from trading, knocked down the boundary pillars, and occupied places on the Indian side of the boundary: and how we had come to revise this Treaty and see that it would be observed in future. They replied that they knew nothing of the Treaty, as it was concluded by the Amban and not by themselves : and they could not be responsible for observing it. I said that that was precisely the reason for our presence here in Tibet. We wished now to make a new Treaty here, where Tibetans themselves could take part in the negotiations, so that they would not in future be able to say that they knew nothing about it. They laughed again and thought this a reasonable argument : but they said that, as it was the Lhasa people and not themselves who had broken the Treaty, we ought to go to Yatung and make the new Treaty there : and they begged me to get leave from the Viceroy to move there and so save the Tashi Lama from trouble. I told them that, in the first place they also had broken the Treaty by crossing the boundary and occupying Giaogong; and, in the second place, we must regard Tibetans as all one people, and hold all responsible for the actions of each. The Tashi Lama must make up his differences with the Lhasa authorities in his own way : and at any rate he could write and say that the English gave no trouble at Khamba Jong for we had taken special care to avoid giving trouble of any sort to the country-people : we had brought everything with us : and we had paid liberally for anything that had been voluntarily brought us for sale. The Deputy hastily replied that it was not we who gave the trouble, but the Chinese and Lhasa officials, who came to negotiate with us and who took everything by force. Little more of importance passed, and on taking leave the Deputy said he would give my message of thanks to the Tashi Lama, and he asked that we would be friendly towards him. I said we had no wish to be anything else : that we had not seen any signs yet of the Tibetans wishing to be friendly to us, but, directly they showed any friendly inclination towards us, they might be sure we would meet them half way. The impression left upon me by this interview is that these Tibetans, though excessively childish, are very pleasant, cheery people and, individually, probably not at all badly disposed towards us. Perhaps, too, these Shigatse people are a trifle less bigoted than their Lhasa brethren. Another point which seemed to be clear from the conversation is that there is considerable friction between the Shigatse and the Lhasa people. And as there is also friction between the Chinese and the Tibetan dele-gates, the party with whom we shall soon commence negotiations are considerably divided amongst themselves.

∞∞⚬⚬∞∞

From Colonel F. E. Younghusband, C.I.E., Khamba Jong, to the Foreign Secretary, Simla, dated Khamba Jong, the 2nd (despatched from Gangtok on 4th) August, 1903. (Telegraphic.)

Persistent rumour of intended attack on us. We are strongly entrenched in open with Maxim, and perfectly ready. Mr. Ho is prepared to bolt, but Tibetan delegate very bumptious and confident.

From the Foreign Secretary, Simla, to Colonel F. E. Younghusband, C.I.E., Gangtok, dated the 5th August, 1903.
(Telegraphic.)

Your telegram, 2nd August, regarding rumours of attack. Do you consider it advisable to employ second Pioneer regiment on improvements to mule track between Raiotdong and Tangu?

From the Foreign Secretary, Simla, to Colonel F. E. Younghusband, C.I.E., Gangtok, dated the 10th August, 1903.
(Telegraphic.)

Before replying to Amban's letter of 24th June, Viceroy will await receipt of official translation of further letter. Please consult Wilton and advise as to replies which should be given, especially as to Amban's status compared with your own rank, and as to suitability of Tibetan and Chinese delegates. If you recommend refusal to recognise those now deputed, please explain clearly of what status Chinese and Tibetans, respectively, should be.

From Colonel F. E. Younghusband, C.I.E., Khamba Jong, to the Foreign Secretary, Simla, dated Khamba Jong, the 8th (despatched from Gantock on 11th) August, 1903.
(Telegraphic.)

Wilton, arrived yesterday evening, thinks Tibetan officials of too low rank, and that Assistant Resident

should represent the Chinese, and a Member of
Council Tibetan Government. In this view I agree.

*Letter from Colonel F. E. Younghusband, C.I.E., British
Commissioner, Tibet Frontier Commission, to the Secretary
to the Government of India, in the Foreign Department,
dated Khamba Jong, the 31st July, 1903.*

I have the honour to submit a despatch, dated the 21st
July, 1903, from the Chinese Resident at Lhasa to His
Excellency the Viceroy. An English translation furnished by Captain Parr is also enclosed. The despatch
is a reply to my letter to the Chinese Resident, a copy
of which was forwarded to you with my letter, dated
the 14th July, 1903.
Annexure.

*Yü, Chinese Imperial Resident at Lhasa, charged with the
administration of Tibetan Affairs Brevet-Lieutenant-
General of the Manchu Brigade, &c., to His Excellency the
Right Honourable Baron Curzon, of Kedleston, P.C.,
G.M.S.I., G.M.I.E., &c., &c., Viceroy and Governor-
General of India, dated Lhasa, Kwang-hsu 29th year, 5th
Inter month, and 27th day [21st July, 1903].*
(Translation)

YOUR EXCELLENCY,
I had received a despatch from Your Excellency's
Frontier Commissioner, Colonel Younghusband.

With regard to deputing representatives for the
discussion of matters, I have already informed Your

Excellency in my despatch, dated the 24th June, 1903, which is on record. I now learn from Colonel Younghusband's despatch that both countries still wish to arrive at a friendly settlement, and have also instructed my Commissioners to act in accordance with this. There is absolutely no truth in the rumour, referred to by Colonel Younghusband, concerning the Dalai Lama's tour in Western Tibet. Up to the present time the Tibetans have refused to hold friendly inter-course with foreigners, and have even rejected all communications from this source. If Colonel Younghusband desires to personally meet the Dalai Lama, it is truly most difficult for me to assist him, which matter I beg Your Excellency to explain to him. Again, Your Excellency's despatch, dated the 3rd June, 1903, states that Your Excellency had appointed Colonel Younghusband, a Resident in your Political department, to proceed to the frontier and discuss and settle matters : now, however, I have received a despatch from Colonel Younghusband in which he describes himself as "British Imperial Resident." I beg Your Excellency kindly to inform me whether Colonel Younghusband is really deputed by Your Excellency, or is he an Imperial Resident appointed by your Government and of equal power to Your Excellency, so that I may be able to communicate with him. I beg Your Excellency's kind consideration of this communication. A necessary despatch.

∘⊶⊰⊱⊷∘

Diary kept by Captain W. F. O'Connor, during the Tibet Frontier Mission.
(Extract.)

26th July, 1903.—Fine morning : some cumulus clouds drifting north. Maximum, temperature, 75.9°; minimum, 42.5°.

Mr. White, accompanied by Captain Bethune and Mr. Bailey, rode out to the Kozo hot springs about 10 a.m. At 11, Mr. Ho's interpreter came into camp with a despatch from the Amban to the Viceroy, in reply to Colonel Younghusband's despatch to the Amban. He gave a verbal translation of the despatch. The Kumar and I then rode out to the Kozo hot springs, where we joined Mr. White, and we all rode back together by a different route, visiting two of local rug factories on the way. We found the valley of the Yaru Chu, when we rode along it, studded with small villages and well cultivated with crops of barley, now in ear and giving a fifty-fold return. The rugs are made by the villagers on a simple form of hand-loom, one man turning out a rug in three to five days. We watched the process of manufacture, and gave a few rupees "buckshish" to the poor people. The temperature of the hottest hot spring at Kozo is 185°, or very nearly boiling point at this elevation. On return to camp we found that Captain Parr, the Chinese Joint Commissioner had arrived. He is staying in a tent provided by Mr. Ho near the Khamba village.

27th July.—Fine morning, but sky overcast with cloud. Maximum temperature 71.9°; minimum 39°.

A day spent in camp without incident. A delegate from Shigatse, a Chang-dzo-pu named Ba-du-la, has arrived at Khamba Jong, and is living in tents near the village.

28th July.—A fine bright morning. Maximum temperature 67.5°; minimum 41°.

The Jongpen and the former Jongpen came into camp about noon, re the matter of the grazing. I had a long conversation with them, and found the Jongpen a better informed man than might be expected. He is acquainted with our form of Government, and asked questions regarding our Members of Parliament, &c.; and he also gave me some information regarding the Lhasa Government, and so on. He is, in fact, very friendly and quite ready to talk when none of the senior officials are about. He says this is an exceptionally dry year. The grazing question was settled to his satisfaction by an agreement to pay a monthly sum for the use of the land.

The 250 Tibetan soldiers coming from Gyangtse for the relief of the Phari garrison reached Taktshong Gompa on the 25th. They were armed only with old-fashioned muskets, swords, and knives. They were under the command of one Rupon and two Gyapon. Half of them have gone on to Phari and half are said still to be halted at Taktshong.

29th July.—A fine bright morning with all the snows showing up clearly. Maximum temperature 73.5°; minimum temperature 36°.

At 12.30 p.m. the Tashi-Chempo delegate Ba–du–la, came into camp bringing presents for the Commissioners. He was received by Colonel Younghusband and Mr. White. Colonel Younghusband began by informing him of the visit of Bogle and Turner to Shigatse at the close of the eighteenth century, and requested him to inform Penchen Rinprehe that their hospitable reception had never been forgotten by the Indian Government. Ba–du–la then spoke on behalf of the Tashi-Chempo Lama, informing the Commissioners that Khamba Jong is a portion of the province of Tsang, and so under Tashi-Chempo, and that the Lhasa Government held Tashi-Chempo responsible for our violation of their territory; and he, therefore, requested that the mission might return to Giaogong. Colonel Younghusband explained that this was impossible, and the matter was debated at some length, as was also the question of the provision of supplies. Finally, the Commissioners' message to the Tashi Lama was repeated, and the delegate withdrew. In conversation with the Kumar of Sikkim afterwards he explained that he had understood the arguments used by us, but that, nevertheless, Tashi-Chempo was held responsible by the Tsong-du or Assembly, for any violation of Tsang territory and is bound to make a protest against our presence, and to do all possible to induce us to withdraw. Neither he nor any of the Tibetans present seemed to have any knowledge regarding the visits to Tashi-Chempo of Bogle and Turner. Ba-du-la is an elderly man of fine presence, who has been for more than twenty years in the service of the Tashi-Chempo Government.

30th July, 1903.—Clear morning. Maximum temperature yesterday 70.5°; minimum last night 36.5°.

At 12 o'clock the Kumar of Sikkim and I rode down to pay a visit to the Tashi-Chempo Treasurer, Ba-du-la, at his tent just beyond the Khamba village. The old gentleman received us in a very friendly manner, and we sat chatting to him for a couple of hours. We brought him down a number of illustrated papers in which he was much interested, especially in portraits of the King and of the Chinese Empress, and he and his friends were delighted with some photographs of Roman Catholic priests and dignitaries, whose dresses reminded them strongly of the Lama vestments of Tibetan monasteries. We took photographs of Ba-du-la and his friends and attendants, and were afterwards entertained at a Tibetan meal consisting of buttered-tea and other delicacies. Politics were avoided, and the conversation was confined to mutual enquiries regarding the customs, government, &c., of England and Tibet.

31st July.—A cloudy morning. There was some rain during the night and the rain gauge registered .12 inches. Maximum temperature 74.9°; minimum 40°.

In the evening two Lachung men, who had been sent to Gyangtse, returned here. They say that the people of the country seem to be in an excited state, and that orders have been sent to Takpo and Kongbo and other provinces for the assembly of soldiers, but that there is no great gathering as yet at Gyangtse. The monks of the three great Lhasa monasteries have professed themselves as ready to march out, if required, but the country people appear to dread their depredations more than they do any movement on our part. The people between here and Gyangtse are burying their household goods and driving their yaks, &c., up into the hills. In fact, as might be expected from our presence here, some little excitement prevails, and there is talk of resorting to arms should negotiations take a wrong turn. Very likely a good deal of this is mere bluster.

The two Tibetan officials had a long interview with Captain Parr to-day.

1st August.—A cloudy morning. Maximum temperature 68.8°; minimum 42°.

2nd August.—A cloudy morning. There was a slight drizzle during the night amounting to .02 inches.

We are having a regular spell of bad weather-sky overcast with heavy clouds and occasional light showers. Maximum temperature 69.2°; minimum 42.5°.

Two Lachung men sent to Shigatse on the 18th July have not returned, and it seems not improbable that they have been stopped by the Tibetans and detained somewhere. I despatched another man, a Tibetan, to Shigatse this morning to see if he can get word of them and to bring back what news he can. The Khamba Jong people keep a very close watch on our camp, and no one can come or go without their knowing of it. Our watcher on the hills above the Jong brings in word this evening that a party of 30 horsemen followed by some 80 to 100 men on foot, with 150 baggage animals, arrived about noon to-day at a small monastery (Utsi), some 4 or 5 miles north of here from the direction of Gyangtse, and were met there by messengers from Khamba Jong and Tinki Jong. They are said to be a party of monks, but their movements for this time of year are somewhat peculiar.

From Colonel F. E. Younghusband, C.I.E., Khamba Jong, to the Foreign Secretary, Simla, dated Khamba Jong, the 10th (despatched from Gangtok on 13th) August, 1903.
(Telegraphic.)

Your telegram, 5 August. White and I think that employment of 2nd Pioneer Regiment on improvement of roads in Sikkim in advisable. Authoritative information has reached me that several meetings of national councillors, of heads of monasteries and officials have been held at Lhasa, and instructions issued to Tibetan delegate here to refuse to negotiate at Khamba Jong, and, if we advance, to oppose us with force. Garrison in Chumbi valley, at Gyantse, and Shigatse have been strengthened, and people throughout the province been ordered to hold themselves in readiness. General attitude of Tibetans is increasingly unfriendly, and is probably due to outside support. Chinese are as unable as in 1886 to keep them in hand.

From the Foreign Secretary, Simla, to Colonel F. E. Younghusband, C.I.E., Gangtok, dated the 15th August, 1903.
(Telegraphic.)

Your telegram, 10th August. Orders being issued to move second Pioneer Regiment, early as possible, to Sikkim.

Diary kept by Captain W. F. O'Connor during the Tibet Frontier Mission.
(Extract.)

3rd August, 1903.—A cloudy morning, .03 inches of rain yesterday. Maximum temperature 65.9°; minimum 40.5°.

The Shigatse officer, Ba-du-la, with the old and the new Jongpens came into camp about noon and were entertained by the Kumar, who showed them pictures and photographs. While they were in camp, Captain Bethune worked the Maxim gun which excited their utmost astonishment and evidently gave them an increased respect for the power of modern armaments. I also showed them the books on Turner's and Bogle's Missions to Tashi-Chempo, which contained pictures of places with which they were well acquainted, and a copy of a Tibetan letter from the Penchen Rinpoche of that time addressed to Turner. After this the Kumar and I entertained them at tiffin, and we parted on very friendly terms. Ba-du-la, I found, has a good acquaintance with the history of Tibet, more especially where it deals with the Gurkha and other campaigns.

Lieutenant W. H. Leonard, I.M.S., arrived from Tangu this afternoon.

4th August.—A lovely clear morning. Maximum temperature 71.8°; minimum 36°.

Mr. White and I, starting at 7.30 a.m., rode northwards along the Shigatse road. Crossing the Kedur La just north of the Jong, we descended into the basin of the Yaru Chu, and crossing a small side stream reached Lung-dong village in the main valley. Lung-dong is a large village (the largest we have seen) situated in a very sheltered valley and surrounded by extensive barley cultivation. Crossing the Yaru Chu by a rough stone bridge, we ascended to the summit of a small pass (the Ta-chen La), passing a little shallow lake (the Chin-chen Tso) en route, and descended again into the broad plain of the Chi Chu, the main source of the Arun. From the top of the Ta-chen La we could see the Shigatse track stretching away due north, passing the large village of Kungma and crossing the central chain by what must be a very easy low pass. What we saw corresponds on the whole very well with the accounts of native explorers. At Kungma barley is said to grow but not to ripen; it is used only as fodder. Wormwood bushes are plentiful as far as we could see, and there are other bushes which could be used as fuel on the summit and northern slopes of the Ta-chen La. In the big Kungma plain there is abundant grazing. Reaching the plain (where some yaks and sheep were grazing), Mr. White and I turned due west, and rode along the flat until at the western edge of the plain we reached the banks of the Chi Chu, which flowing from the mountains to the north and north-east runs past Kungma, and skirts the western edge of the plain. It is a sluggish stream, averaging some 50 to 60 feet in width and two or three in depth and with dirty discoloured water. It evidently carries down a quantity of disintegrated material from the southern slopes of the central chain. Near its exit from the plain some 40 yaks were grazing. The grazing is good and the western surface of the plain well watered. The Chi Chu now runs down a narrow gorge with hills rising some few hundred feet on either bank. We followed the stream down a well-marked path to its exit on to another wide maidan some two to three miles further west. Still following the stream we passed the large village of Gye-dong surrounded by barley cultivation. Here we met a party of monks from Utsi Gompa, who were out on an expedition to levy supplies from the villagers. Turning south we crossed a low pass, and passing close to Utsi Gompa we reached Khamba Jong at 5 p.m.

It is worth noting that we passed two companies of traders during the day-both going to Phari. The first party near Lung-dong were carrying salt to Phari from Shigatse; and the second, which we passed in the gorge of the Chi Chu, were bringing in mustard oil from Chib-lung (north-west of Dobta). Various tracks from this part of the country converge at Phari-the recognised trade mart. Khamba Jong lies altogether away from the regular trade routes.

The Kumar of Sikkim visited the Utsi Gompa during the day, but was refused admittance. It is said that some official or person of importance has arrived there, but we are unable to ascertain who it is.

The climate at present is delightful. Mild and warm like the pleasantest summer weather at home.

A four-foot breastwork of sods and stones has

been completed round the camp with an exterior ditch and flanking defences at the four corners and entrance. The exits are closed by barbed-wire gates at night.

5th August.—Fine morning, but sky clouded. Maximum temperature 74.5°; min.mum 37.5°.

A quiet day in camp. A constant stream of supplies keeps coming to the Jong from the surrounding country, and messengers continually pass to and fro, day and night. The two Tibetan officers still remain shut up in the Jong, and we have no communication with them whatever.

From Colonel F. E. Younghusband, C.I.E., Khamba Jong, to the Foreign Secretary, Simla, dated Khamba Jong, the 15th [despatched from Nyema (Sikkim) on 17th] August, 1903.
(Telegraphic.)

I have despatched 10th August official translation of Amban's reply to despatch, 31st July. I have consulted Wilton, and advise that Viceroy should reply to Amban's letter that he does not appear to have recognised the importance which Viceroy attaches to present negotiations, nor the high rank the Commissioner, who is entitled to deal and correspond directly with Amban in same way as Consul-General and Consul deal with Provincial Governor and Governor-General in China; that it is most important that he should so deal directly with

Amban; that delegates now appointed are not of sufficiently high rank to negotiate with British Commissioners; and that Associate Resident, sometimes known as Assistant Resident, should be deputed to represent Chinese, and a Councillor, the Tibetans.

Diary kept by Captain W. F. O'Connor during the Tibet Frontier Mission.
(Extract.)

6th August, 1903.—Dull cloudy morning. Maximum temperature 75.5°; minimum 37.5°.

There is a rumour this morning to the effect that the two Lachung men who have been detained at Shigatse have been beaten as well as imprisoned. From all we know regarding Tibetan methods of administering justice, this is more than probable. Two small military officers (Ding-pon or, as they are generally called here, Ske-ngo) arrived at the Jong this morning from Shigatse. It appears that there has been some question of supplying the two Tibetan officers with an escort of similar strength to ours, and that these men actually started, but were stopped by the request of the officials themselves. They are now halted near Rke on the other side of the mountains on the Shigatse road. These Ding-pon have come to ask for instructions. It has been arranged that Mr. White is to call on Chinese Commissioners to-morrow re the detention at Shigatse of the Lachung men, and the Tibetan Commissioners have also been requested to be present.

7th August.—Dull cloudy morning. Maximum temperature 72.8°; minimum 39.9°.

Two men returned from a tour round the Sikkim frontier report that the troops in Chumbi, who were relieved a few days ago by 250 fresh men, are still in the valley, but are expected at Ta-tsang Gompa in a few days. At present there is double garrison in Chumbi. They say all the passes round about are being watched, and that they were followed here from near Ta-tsang by two Tibetans.

At 12.30 Mr. White and I rode down to Captain Parr's camp where Mr. White was met by Captain Parr, Ho, and the Tung-yig-Chembo-the De-pon being indisposed. Mr. White referred to the report that two British subjects had been caught and imprisoned at Shigatse, and begged that enquiries might be set on foot by the Tibetan authorities, and that the men might be returned to Khamba within ten days. The Tung-yig-Chembo said he had no cognisance of the matter, but that he would make enquiries; and he said that ten days was not sufficient for an enquiry to be made, and he requested a longer time. Mr. White, however, insisted upon a minimum period of ten days and closed the interview. The Tung-yig-Chembo was obviously uneasy throughout. There can be little doubt that he is perfectly well acquainted with all the facts of the case. But he made no promise to comply with Mr. White's wishes in the matter, or to secure the release of the two Lachung men. He argued that they were well aware that they were not allowed to go to Shigatse. In reply to this, we pointed out to him that if this were so, the men should have been stopped and turned back, but that their imprisonment and possible punishment was an unjustifiable proceeding as between two friendly nations.

Mr. Wilton of the Chinese Consular Service arrived here this evening from Tangu after a long journey from Chungking.

Late in the evening a letter written in Chinese and Tibetan was received from Mr. Ho.

8th August.—Clear morning. Maximum temperature 69°; minimum 36.5°. .06 inches of rain yesterday.

Mr. Ho's letter was merely a protest written on behalf of the Tibetans to say that ten days was not sufficient to conduct their enquiries regarding the Lachung men and requesting more time. The letter was returned to Captain Parr, at his request, as it had been written without his knowledge or sanction. A young Tibetan sent to Shigatse on the 1st returned this morning with the news that the Lachung men have certainly been captured and imprisoned, and that he hears they have been beaten once.

9th August.—Horizon clear to the south. Clouds overhead; maximum temperature 74.5°; minimum 36.2°.

News received this morning that all our milk-yaks which had been grazing in a valley near by have disappeared in the night, together with the two yak herds. The yaks were not our property, but belonged to some Phari men, who have evidently been frightened away. All they left behind were our two milk-cans lying in the middle of the maidan. I have sent to try and find out what has become of them. The Sikkim men who were living in the village here have been turned out by their landlord as he is afraid to harbour them any longer. Captain Parr returned Ho's letter with a translation of the Chinese copy.

10th August, 1903.—Dull cloudy morning. .08_ of rain yesterday. Maximum temperature 72.5°; minimum 41.5°.

11th August.—Cloudy morning. .022 rain yesterday. Maximum temperature 72°; minimum 42°.

Mr. White and I, starting at 8 a.m. and accompanied by the Kumar of Sikkim, rode out almost due west across the Khamba Jong plain (called the Chumo Tang). After about four miles we reached the valley of a stream which, flowing from the snows of the Sikkim frontier towards the north, fertilises a wide bed in this arid country. It is the same stream on which I halted for one night in my exploration of this country in 1896. The bed of the stream is wide and grassy, varying from quarter to three-quarters of a mile in width, and there are three or four villages dotted here and there, wide grassy and rushy pastures, and some very fine barley cultivation. Following down the left side of this valley, we reached after about a mile or so the junction of this stream with the main valley of the Yaru Chu or Amu, which likewise flows in a wide grassy bed with villages and cultivation at intervals. The Yaru Chu, where we reached it, turns due west, and flowing through on rather narrow gorge, debouches into the wide plain of Tinki Jong just beyond. Climbing one of the side-hills of the gorge, we had a fine view of the Tinki Jong plain to the west. The river, leaving the gorge, turns to the right (northwards), and skirting the northern slopes bounding the plain, flows in a wide semi-circle passing the Tinki Jong and other villages, and runs away due west, where it enters another narrow ravine bounded by high hills on each side, and so disappears from view. It afterwards turns south into Nepal. The northern half of the Tinki plain, where watered by the Amu, is grassy and fertile, but the southern half is dry, bare, and arid. It is crossed, however, by two small streams flowing from the Sikkim frontier, in the bed of each of which is one village. The distance from Khamba Jong to our point of observation is about nine miles, and this stretch of country is the barest we have traversed. From within about one mile of the Jong to as far as we could see westwards the country is absolutely bare-even the small wormwood bushes, which we are using here as fuel, ceasing entirely. Similarly with the country to the south. But even this desolate country can support sheep and goats, of which we saw several large flocks numbering several hundred each; and in the valleys of the stream, yaks, cows, mules, ponies and donkeys were grazing. The country, in fact, is by no means so barren and devoid of 'supplies as a first view would incline one to suppose. Heavy rain came on about 1 p.m., and we rode hastily back to camp.

Mr. Bailey took out a small reconnoitring patrol of three mounted sepoys and two Sikkim men, and rode out to Kungmo on the shigatse road. The two Sikkim men were sent on ahead, and were stopped, as before, by the villagers, but the patrol then rode through the village and for some little distance beyond, meeting with no other interference than protests from the people.

Rain fell steadily all the afternoon and evening.

12th August.-A dark, cloudy morning. Rain fell during the night, and .592 was registered. Maximum temperature 68.5°; minimum 40°. Some little damage has been done to the Jong by the rain. In one place the stones which formed the foundation on the rock have fallen away, leaving a large gap. The whole of the old building is full of great cracks and must be very insecure. The Teling Kusho called again on the Kumar to-day, and I had a long conversation with him. He is a very interesting man fat and good natured and most talkative. Like most of the Tsang people, he cordially dislikes and fears the Lhasa Government. He gave me some interesting details regarding the parts of Tibet he has visited and some information about the semi-independent district of Po-yul, which he tells me has now submitted to Lhasa influence. There are three Chiefs in Po-yul he tells me, one of whom, a stiff-necked ruffian, always upheld his independence. He, however, died a few years ago, and since then the country has been subordinated to Lhasa. The country is famous for its supply of musk. He also gave me some information regarding the method of collecting the revenue of the country, which appears to vary in every province and almost in every district. His own little estate at Teling is rent-free. He shears his sheep next month, and the wool is all made into blankets and clothing : he has practically none surplus for export. What little trade he does is with the Walloong people of Eastern Nepal, who bring in dyes and some cloths from Darjeeling, and exchange them for the woolleus of the country. He tells me that he, in common with all the inhabitants of this part of Tibet, practically hibernate during the winter. The winds, he says, are fearfully cold, and the air full of sand and dust. No one ever emerges from his house unless obliged to.

I hear from some Sikkim men that the relieved garrison of Phari is now on its way back towards Gyantse, but the information is rather doubtful. There are still a couple of tents and some half dozen Tibetans at Giaogong.

Mr. Shen, Mr. Ho's interpreter, has been dismissed, and leaves here for Yatung in a day or two.

A light rain fell during the whole day.

Letter from His Excellency the Viceroy and Governor-General of India to His Excellency Yu, Chinese Imperial Resident at Lhasa, Brevet-Lieutenant-General of the Manchu Brigade, dated Simla, the 25th August, 1903.

I have the honour to acknowledge the receipt, on the 2nd August, of Your Excellency's letter, dated the 24th June, 1903, replying to my despatch of the 3rd June. I am much pleased to learn from your communication that you are so sincerely desirous that the questions at issue should be discussed and settled in a friendly spirit.

You inform me that on your part you have deputed Mr. Ho, a civil official of the third rank, and Commissioner Parr, who holds the third class of the Imperial Order of the Double Dragon : you observe that these officers are truly of equal rank with the British Commissioners. On this point I fear that Your Excellency is under some misconception. You are already aware of the great importance of the matters now before us, and of the desirability of settling them without delay, before they have developed into complications of serious gravity. In view, moreover, of the fact that in December, 1902, the Wai-wu-pu had written to His Britannic Majesty's Chargé d'Affaires at Peking that the Chinese Government, attaching deep importance to international relations and regarding this question as of great importance, had specially appointed Yu Tai to proceed with all speed and negotiate with Mr. White, who at that time was the highest British officer concerned, I deemed it advisable to appoint as the British representative an officer both of high rank and of special experience and ability. Colonel Younghusband, whom I selected for the purpose with the concurrence of the Government of His Majesty the King-Emperor, is, as I previously explained, a Resident in the Political Department of the Government of India and also a Colonel in the Indian Army, and, as such, an officer of far higher status than the Chinese Commissioners, neither of whom is, in my opinion, qualified either by his official position or by his diplomatic experience to take the principal part in these weighty discussions. His Excellency Yu Tai has not yet, I understand, reached Lhasa, and it is possible that some delay may occur before he is able to confer with Colonel Younghusband. Pending his arrival, I have little doubt that your own participation in the negotiations would be the surest means of paving the way to a friendly and satisfactory settlement; failing that, however, I feel sure that on further consideration Your Excellency will agree with me in thinking that the only other Chinese official in Tibet, who can suitably be charged with the important function of conferring with the British representatives, is the Assistant Amban, who is associated with you as your colleague.

As regards the Tibetan representatives, you inform me that the Dalai Lama, at your request, has deputed his Chief Secretary, Lo-Pu-Ts'ang Ch'Êng Lo, and Wang-ch'ü Chieh-Pu, Depon of Lhasa. I am obliged to you for so readily acceding to my proposal that your delegates should be accompanied by envoys from the Tibetan Government. But in the case of these officials also, their rank is neither equal with that of the British Commissioners, nor appropriate to the negotiations in hand. Apart, moreover, from the question of their status, the Tibetan representatives have, by their behaviour during the short period since their arrival at Khamba Jong, shown themselves entirely unsuited for diplomatic intercourse. I will not weary

Your Excellency with accounts of the many instances of their discourtesy and obstructiveness which have been reported to me, but I may mention, as evidence of their unfitness, that when on the second day after his arrival Colonel Younghusband proposed to hand to them a memorandum explanatory of the previous relations between India and Tibet and of the questions now at issue, these Tibetan envoys professed themselves unable even to accept the document. With such persons negotiations are impossible; I feel confident that you will at once recognise the necessity of substituting for them more suitable delegates; and I would suggest, for your consideration, that the Tibetan Government should be invited to depute a Councillor of the Dalai Lama accompanied by a high member of the National Assembly.

As regards the place of negotiation, I am at a loss to understand the objections raised by Your Excellency to the selection of Khamba Jong which, I understood, was considered suitable by you. At any rate, I am unable to hold out any hope of the withdrawal of the British Commissioners from that place, so long as the Tibetans maintain their present unfriendly and impracticable attitude. During the present season of the year the climate at Khamba Jong is agreeable, and it is, as I have already explained, the nearest point in Tibet to the disputed boundary. It is impossible for our officers to stay on the mountain top where that boundary lies. Besides, the present negotiations must be conducted in Tibet, as the former Convention which the Tibetans have repudiated was concluded in India, and His

Majesty's Government are not prepared to allow a sim-ilar repudiation of any agreement at which we may now arrive. The winter is, however, approaching and, unless very early steps are taken to complete the pre-sent negotiations, it may be necessary for my Commissioners to select some other place in Tibet for passing the winter, as Colonel Younghusband has been informed by your representatives that the climate of Khamba Jong during that season is unsuitable.

In addition to your letter of the 24th June, I have also received your communication of the 21st July, in which, in reply to a letter from Colonel Younghusband, you write to me enquiring as to that officer's position. I regret that, in view of my previous assurance as to Colonel Younghusband's high rank, you should have treated him so discourteously as to refuse to reply to his letter and to question his status. I may remind Your Excellency that in China it is the custom for British Consuls to correspond direct with Viceroys of Provinces, and I am sure that, when you consider this fact in connection with my preceding remarks regarding the rank of Colonel Younghusband, together with the circumstance that the Government of His Majesty the King-Emperor have deputed as his assistant and subordinate Mr. Wilton, an officer who has recently held the post of Consul in China, you will at once recognise that the British Commissioner is entitled to expect not only that you will reply to his communications, but also that in every other respect you will co-operate with him in the most cordial manner possible.

I have, &c.,
(Signed) CURZON,
Viceroy and Governor-General of India.

Letter from the Under-Secretary to the Government of India, in the Foreign Department, to Colonel F. E. Young-husband, C.I.E., British Commissioner, Tibet Frontier Commission, dated Simla, the 26th August, 1903.

With reference to your letters, dated the 27th July, 1903 and the 31st July, 1903, I am directed to forward the enclosed letter from His Excellency the Viceroy to His Excellency Yu, Chinese Imperial Resident at Lhasa, and to request that, if you see no objection it may be transmitted to the Amban with the least possible delay.

From Major G. H. Bretherton, Gangtok, to the Foreign Secretary, Simla, dated the 24th August, 1903.
(Telegraphic.)

I have asked Colonel Younghusband where second regiment for Sikkim should be located.

From the Foreign Secretary, Simla, to Major G. H. Bretherton, Gangtok, dated the 28th August, 1903.
(Telegraphic.)

Your telegram, 24th August. Second Pioneer Regiment will be employed on repairing road leading to the Jelap Pass.

Diary kept by Captain W. F. O'Connor during the Tibet Frontier Mission.
(Extract.)

13th August, 1903.—Still very cloudy. .32 of rain yesterday. Maximum temperature 60.5°; minimum 38.5°.

I rode down to Captain Parr's camp after breakfast in order to ask him to try and secure the services for us of a man who can speak both Tibetan and Chinese. Mr. Wilton's Chinese writer can speak nothing but his own language, and is badly in need of some intermediary between himself and the other clerks and servants in the camp, most of whom speak Tibetan. Captain Parr promised to do what he could in the matter.

The Jongpen has sent his wife away, and is despatching his personal property as fast as he can to his house at Tse-gang near Shigatse. The villagers are said to be burying their belongings.

14th August.—A cloudy morning. Maximum temperature yesterday 62.5°; minimum 40°.

Shen, Mr. Ho's English-speaking interpreter, who has been dismissed, called to say good-bye about 8 o'clock. He took his departure from the village about 10 o'clock in great state. Before starting he sent a dozen Chinese soldiers to line up on the road before our camp, who saluted as he rode past, himself arrayed in a scarlet gown and smoking a large cigar. His object was presumably to show us that he was not leaving in disgrace. He goes to Yatung. About 1 o'clock I rode down with Mr. Wilton to call on Mr. Ho, who received us in one of his tents. Captain Parr also was present. Mr. Wilton conversed for some time with Mr. Ho in Chinese. There appears to be a difficulty in procuring the services of a Tibetan and Chinese-speaking servant. The Tibetans are so suspicious that no one cares to enter our service, and Mr. Ho does not wish to commit himself by sending us a man.

A Tibetan returned from Dingri (a fort to the north of the Nepal frontier to the west of here) reports the usual garrison of 500 soldiers at Dingri, but he says that orders have been issued for the collection of a considerable force (which he puts at 3,000) between us and Shigatse. Other informants also report a gathering on the Shigatse road, and steps are being taken to ascertain its strength.

15th August.—Sky a bit clearer this morning. Maximum temperature 67.5°; minimum 39.5°.

The mule belonging to Mr. White's Munshi was stolen during the night by a Tibetan, who rode off with it towards Shigatse. Fortunately he was met on the road by a man in our employment, who recognised the mule, and rescued it and brought it back to camp.

My Tibetan clerk paid a visit to Badula, the Shigatse Treasury Officer, to-day, and had a long conversation with him. Badula told him that the Tsong-du, or Assembly, have written to the Tashi-Chempo Government to complain that they have not taken proper measures to induce us to return to the frontier, and instructing them to despatch an officer of high rank to remonstrate with us. He read over to the clerk a copy of the Tsong-du's letter, the concluding paragraph of which was to the effect that the contents have been communicated, for information, to the Ka-sha, or Council of Four Shapes, showing that the orders of the Tsong-du are issued without any reference to the Council, and are merely communicated to them for information, and not for their advice or consent. This bears out the information I had already received that it is not usual for the Shapes to sit in the Tsong-du, although they would appear occasionally to do so in special cases. Badula also complained of the helpless attitude assumed by Ho. An intermediary, he said, should be a powerful man carrying weight with both parties, whereas Ho is a person of no consequence. This observation throws some light upon the view which the Tibetans take of the Chinese Commissioners. They appear to value their services rather as those of middlemen than of the representatives of a powerful nation whose councils necessarily have an intrinsic importance.

16th August.—Fine bright morning. Maximum temperature 70.9°; minimum 38°.

Captain Parr came to our camp about noon. Mr. White rode up the Khamba Jong nulla, where he shot a kyang, which is being brought into camp. It is reported that there are 12 Tibetan soldiers still at the Tsolamo lakes inside the Sikkim frontier just north of the Donkhya Pass, and six or eight at Giaogong.

17th August, 1903.—Cloudy morning. Maximum temperature 68.5°; minimum 36.5°

It appears that the man who rescued and brought back the Munshi's mule, according to his own account, was in reality the person who had walked off with it. The two kyangs shot up the Khamba Jong nulla were brought into camp and skinned. The ten days allowed the Tibetans to produce the two Lachung men from Shigatse have elapsed to-day, and there is no sign of the men. I sent out three Lachung men to reconnoitre towards Kongma.

18th August.—There was a little rain during the night and lasting up till 8.30 this morning; 0.1 inch registered. Maximum temperature 70.5°; minimum 40.5°.

Mr. White sent a letter addressed to the Chinese and Tibetan Commissioners to inform them that the ten days allowed for the production of the Sikkim men had elapsed, asking what steps they proposed to take in the matter, and requesting a reply by evening. About noon the Tashi-chempo officials rode into Khamba village. They consist of a young Abbot, an incarnate Lama, of some 30 years of age, deputed by the Pencheu Rinpoche (Tashi Lama) to visit us and request our return to the frontier. His name is Tu-wang Tulku (Tulku means "incarnation"), and he is abbot of the Ngak-je section of the Tashi-Chempo monastery-one of the four sections into which that monastery is divided. He is accompanied by his steward, or Di-chung-wa, a tsi-dung or ecclesiastical official, an elderly man of the Fifth rank. He comes as the representative of the monk element. There are also two lay officials with the party, one of the Fifth and one of the Sixth rank. They represent the lay officials and lay general public. So the four officials represent between them all classes of Tibetan society-spiritual, official, and private. They have requested to be allowed to call on the British Commissioners as soon as possible. The three men sent to Kongma have returned with the news that, besides the usual villagers, there are some 20 Tibetan soldiers in the village.

19th August.—A little rain last night; .02 inches registered. Cloudy morning. Maximum temperature 60°; minimum 41°.

A letter was sent by Mr. White, addressed to the Chinese and Tibetan Commissioners, saying that, as no reply had been received to his communication of the day before, he demanded an indemnity of Rs. 1,000 each for the two Lachung men detained at Shigatse, and reiterated his demand for their prompt production at Khamba Jong. At the same time a letter was despatched to Colonel Brander, Commanding at Tangu, requesting him to take steps to at once turn out any Tibetans occupying positions at Giaogong and Tso-lamo, and to seize live-stock, the property of Tibetans making use of grazing lands within the Sikkim frontier, to the value of Rs. 2,000.

About 10 a.m. the Teling Kusho called on the camp, and was, as usual, very communicative. He imparted a number of details regarding the Tashi-Chempo officials who had arrived the day before, and on other minor points; as to political topics he could only tell me that our prolonged stay in Tibetan territory was exciting more and more suspicion amongst Tibetans of all classes, and that no day passed without absurdly exaggerated rumours being circulated in every bazar in the country-and the further the rumour travelled the more it grew. The Kumar and I asked him to bring some of his friends to lunch with us, and he presently re-appeared with Badula, the old Jongpen, and one of the newly-arrived lay officers-a quiet middle-aged man named Teng-ba. We showed them the gramophone, picture papers, and so on, and took their photographs. They are especially pleased with my little Kodak photographs, and begged for copies for themselves and their friends. We then had tiffin and parted on very friendly terms with mutual good-wishes.

Colonel Younghusband sent a letter to Mr. Ho, requesting him to procure the immediate withdrawal of any Tibetans occupying positions in Sikkim territory at Giaogong, Tso-lamo, and Lho-nak.

We are still purchasing grain and hiring grazing at very high rates from the Jongpen. But all the animals are fit and in good condition.

Letter from Colonel F. E. Younghusband, C.I.E., British Commissioner, Tibet Frontier Commission, to the Secretary to the Government of India, in the Foreign Department, dated Khamba Jong, the 19th August, 1903.

I have the honour to report, for the information of the Government of India, that two Sikkim (Lachung) men, who had proceeded to Shigatse to trade, were seized by the Tibetan authorities about four weeks ago, and the headman of the district to which they belonged reported to Mr. White, the Political Officer in Sikkim, that they had been severely beaten by the Tibetan authorities and detained in custody, and he asked for measures to be taken for their release. Mr. White made enquiries of the local authorities, but they professed themselves ignorant of the where-abouts of these men. He therefore called on Mr. Ho personally, and demanded that the men should be produced within ten days. Messrs. Ho and Parr wrote to Mr. White and myself, asking for an extension of the term. A copy of their letter and our reply I have the honour to enclose. We informed them that I was in entire accord with Mr. White that ten days was ample time for the purpose.

No reply was received by the end of ten days. On the eleventh day Mr. White asked if any reply was to be expected, and being informed that the Tibetans were unable to get information regarding the two men, he has to-day demanded from the Tibetans compensation to the amount of Rs. 2,000, and pend-ing the receipt of this sum has made arrangements for the seizure of Tibetan sheep in Sikkim territory of equivalent value to that amount.

Though Mr. White has acted in consultation with me in this matter, I have been anxious, as far as possi-ble, to keep this as a matter between him, as the

Political Officer in Sikkim, and the local Tibetan authorities in this province. If, however, as appears likely, the Lhasa Government and not the Shigatse local authorities, are responsible for this unfriendly act, I will inform you, as the Government of India may wish to take more special notice of the case.

That the men have actually been seized and beaten there is no doubt, the information having reached us from several sources. A missionary lady in Lachung has also forwarded an appeal to Mr. White on behalf of the sister of one of the men to help her.

The action of the Tibetans is the more unjustifiable, because I have taken no notice of the number of Tibetans who have been coming into Sikkim lately, although it had been reported to me that they had come to spy our military movements and even to destroy bridges. We could watch our bridges, and as for military information the more of it they obtained the better.

Now, however, I have informed Mr. Ho that the Tibetans must be withdrawn from the Giaogong valley, and I have taken steps to see that they are withdrawn.

Annexure.

(TRANSLATION.)

To Colonel F. E. Younghusband, C.I.E., and Mr. White, Imperial British Commissioners.

At the interview held to-day with Mr. White concerning the arrest of some Lachen men at Shigatse, the Tibetan officers were informed that the arrested men are to be produced within ten days, and failing this the British authorities will take the matter into their own hands. But the Tung-yig-Chempo did not undertake to do so within the specified period. He asked why these Lachen men proceeded to Shigatse, and where they were arrested, he being truly unaware, After Mr. White's departure from interview, the Tibetan officers were made fully to understand that this matter must be settled in a friendly spirit, and the Tibetan officers replied that they wished to be friendly and would send a letter to Shigatse, and enquire as to these men's arrival there, and also concerning the truth of their arrest. On the receipt of reply, I will inform you.

At the time of the Lachen men's departure for Shigatse, the British authorities did not notify me and the Tibetan officers. Moreover, in accordance with old custom, Lachen men are prohibited from proceeding to Shigatse : formerly these men attempted to do so, but were stopped, which is on record. Now the British authorities have been informed of the arrest of these Lachen men, so the Tibetan authorities must write and enquire into the matter, and then we will be able to discuss and settle the question. I fear, however, that the period allowed (ten days) is not sufficient. I hope, therefore, as our relations are most friendly, that you will wait a few days longer until the Tibetan officers have ascertained the facts : a repiy must be received in, at the most, a little over ten days.

Cards of HO KUANG-HSIEH and PARR.

Dated Khamba Jong, Kwang Hou,

29th year, 6th Moon, and 15th day (7th Angust, 1903).

P.S.—As you possess a Tibetan linguist, I therefore send copies of this letter in Chinese and Tibetan, and beg you kindly to send your reply in English and Tibetan, so that I may hand a copy of the latter to Tibetan officials.

Colonel Younghusband and Mr. White have the honour to acknowledge the receipt of the memorandum, dated 7th August, from Mr. Ho and Captain Parr, the Imperial Chinese Commissioners.

They are unaware of any old custom by which Sikkim men are prohibited from proceeding to Shigatse. According to their information, Sikkim men have from old time been in the custom of visiting Shigatse in the same way as Shigatse men visit Sikkim. There are Shigatse men now visiting Sikkim without any let or hindrance from the British authorities : and Colonel Younghusband was in entire agreement with Mr. White, the Political Officer in Sikkim, when he made the demand that the two Lachen men under his protection, who had been detained at Shigatse against their will, should be produced within ten days. Colonel Younghusband considers the time allowed is ample, as a messenger can reach Shigatse in two days easily. He cannot, therefore, consent to any prolongation of the period : and he trusts that Mr. Ho will make the Tibetan officials realise the serious nature of their offence against international usage and courtesy in detaining against their will persons under the protection of the British Government.

F. E. YOUNGHUSBAND.

J. C. WHITE.

The 10th August, 1903.

Letter from Colonel F. E. Younghusband, C.I.E., British Commissioner, Tibet Frontier Commission, to the Secretary to the Government of India, in the Foreign Department, dated Khamba Jong, the 20th August, 1903.

In continuation of my letter of yesterday's date, I have the honour to forward two petitions received this morning from the relatives of the two men who have been seized.

It will be observed that they entertain no doubt of the men having been seized and ill-treated; and also that they consider that Lachung men have a right to trade at Shigatse.

Annexure 1.

Letter from Gonpu of Lachung, to J. C. White, Esq., Political Officer, Sikkim, and Joint Commissioner, Tibet Frontier Commission, dated Khamba Jong, the 20th August, 1903.

I most humbly and respectfully beg to bring to your Honour's kind notice that my brother, Dajom, went to Shigatse for trading purposes some time ago, and now I have heard from reliable source that he has been captured, thrashed, and put in prison by the Tibetan authorities there.

I am quite ignorant of the reasons why he was captured and put in prison, as the Lachen and Lachung people are in the habit of going into Tibet for exchange of trade.

I and the other members of the family noted on the margin solely depend on him for living, he being the responsible male person in the family.I do not know what has been done with my brother by the Tibetans by this time.

Under these circumstances, I pray for the immediate release of my brother through your favour, as we are the subject of the British Government, and for which act of your Honour's kindness I shall ever pray.

Annexure 2.

Letter from Sonamdohua, sister of Kingaduda, to J. C. White, Esq., Political Officer, Sikkim, and Joint Commissioner, Tibet Frontier Commission, dated the 20th August, 1903.

I most humbly and respectfully beg to bring to your Honour's kind notice that my brother, Kingaduda, went to Shigatse for trading purposes some time ago, and now I have heard from reliable source that he has been captured, thrashed, and put in prison by the Tibetan authorities there.

I am quite ignorant of the reasons why he was captured and put in prison, as the Lachen and Lachung people are in the habit of going into Tibet for exchange of trade.

I and the other members of the family noted in

the margin solely depend on him for living, he being the only responsible male person in the family. I do not know what has been done with my brother by the Tibetans by this time.

Under these circumstances, I pray for the immediate release of my brother through your favour, as we are the subject of the British Government, and for which act of kindness I shall ever pray.

From the Resident in Nepal, Segowlie, to the Foreign Secretary, Simla, dated the 31st August, 1903.
(Telegraphic.)

Maharaja offers five hundred yaks at once and eight thousand within one month for transport for Tibet Mission.

From the Foreign Secretary, Simla, to Colonel F. E. Younghusband, C.I.E., Khamba Jong, dated the 2nd September, 1903.
(Telegraphic.)

Your action concerning Lachung men is approved, and Tibetans should be informed that, unless immediate reparation is made, we shall exact such restitution as we think fit. Nepal Minister has offered us 500 yaks at once, and 8,000 within month. Arrival of some of these with Nepalese officer by Tinki Jong might have good effect. How many would you desire? If no reply is received from Amban to Viceroy's letter at early date, and if Tibetans continue impracticable, it

will be desirable that you should submit proposals for
dealing with matter, and should contemplate winter
arrangements. It may be necessary for you to investi-
gate neighbourhood of Khamba Jong for suitable
winter camp. Second battalion of Pioneers has been
ordered to Sikkim directly after rains, and will work
on route to Jelap.

*Letter from Colonel F. E. Younghusband, C.I.E., British
Commissioner, Tibet Frontier Commission, to the Secretary
to the Government of India, in the Foreign Department,
dated Khamba Jong, the 21st August, 1903.*
(Extract.)

I have the honour to report that to-day the head
Abbot of the Tashi Lampo Monastery, two monks,
and a lay representative, together with the Deputy
from the Tashi Lama, who had formerly visited me,
and the present and past Jongpens (District officers)
of Khamba Jong called upon me to make a further
formal representation, on behalf of the Tashi Lama of
Tashi Lampo (Shigatse), against our presence in the
province under his administration. After I had made
enquiries after His Holiness's health, and informed
the Abbot what a pleasure it was to me to make the
acquaintance of so distinguished a person as the head
of one of the great monasteries of Tibet, the Abbot
made his formal representation, which was repeated,
I may say, at one time or other during the course of
the interview by each member of his staff. He said it
was not usual to send the head Abbot of a monastery

on a mission of this kind, but, in view of the importance of the matter, the Tashi Lama had held a Council at which it had been decided to send him and representatives of the official and unofficial communities to represent his views to me, so that what he was now about to say were the words of the Tashi Lama himself. The representation was this. Each province was held responsible by the Lhasa Government for keeping foreigners from crossing the frontier, so the Lhasa authorities were now blaming the Shigatse authorities for allowing us to cross the frontier; and still more were they being blamed for allowing us to cross with armed soldiers. The Tashi Lama, therefore, hoped that, as we professed to be here with entirely friendly intentions, we would show our friendship to him by retiring to either Giaogong or Yatung and carrying on the negotiations there. In reply, I told the Abbot that the reason for our coming here had been explained by the Viceroy to the Amban, and by Mr. White and myself to Mr. Ho, to the Lhasa delegates here, and to the Tashi Lama's former Deputy. I would, however, out of courtesy to His Holiness repeat them again. They were very simple. It was obvious the negotiations had to take place either in Tibetan territory or in British territory. When the treaty was originally made, the Chinese Amban came down to British territory, but after its conclusion the Tibetans said they knew nothing about it. On the present occasion, therefore, the Viceroy decided that it would be best that the negotiations should take place in Tibet itself, and His Excellency informed the

Amban that he had decided upon sending Mr. White and me to Khamba Jong, because it was the nearest inhabited place to that part of the frontier about which questions had arisen. As to our having come with armed soldiers, such an escort as we had was only what was customary with officers of high rank, and the number we had brought was considerably less than the number which the Amban took to Calcutta. I said that sorry though I was not to be able to meet the wishes of His Holiness, I could only answer him that, as I had been given no really satisfactory reason why we should withdraw which I could submit to His Excellency the Viceroy as just cause why he should reconsider his decision, I must tell him quite clearly and decidedly that there was no prospect whatever of our withdrawing from Khamba Jong till the frontier matters in question had been discussed. Whether we might go elsewhere for the discussion of trade matters was a question for future consideration. The Abbot then said that the objection to our being at Khamba Jong was that it was outside the disputed region, whereas Giaogong was inside it, and, therefore, a more suitable place for the discussion, and he asked that the Tashi Lama's representation might be transmitted to the Viceroy. I replied that I would, of course, report to His Excellency what the Abbot had represented to me on behalf of the Tashi Lama; but that we did not admit that there was any doubt at all as to the position of the frontier. It was most clearly laid down in the Treaty. We understood, however, that the Tibetans wished to regain certain lands round

Giaogong which they claimed had once belonged to them, and about that we were prepared to negotiate. "But," I asked the Abbot, "when one man has a certain thing which another man wishes to get from him, which is the wisest course for the second man to pursue? To make friends with him or to do everything he can to make him annoyed"? The Tibetans all burst out laughing at this; and I then went on to say that the Lhasa authorities instead of doing everything they could to dispose us favourably towards them and incline us to make concessions to them in regard to the Giaogong lands had adopted a steadily unfriendly attitude; they had sent only small officials to meet Mr. White and me, though the Viceroy, in view of the importance of the matter, had asked that the highest should be sent; and these small officials did nothing but tell me that they would not negotiate anywhere else but at Giaogong. This was not the way to predispose me in their favour. The Abbot replied that the delegates were not small officials, but were next in rank to the Shapi (Councillors). I said I had concluded they were men of little power, because when I had made a speech to them on my first arrival and had asked them to report the substance of it to the Lhasa Government, they had refused. If they could not even report a speech, I concluded they could not be fit to negotiate an important treaty. The Abbot then suggested that, as we could not go back to Giaogong, we might go back to the Serpebu La. I told him I thought that about the most inhospitable suggestion that had ever been made to me in any country; that there was neither grass, fuel, nor water there, and it was a pass 17,000 feet high. The Abbot said he had not seen the place himself, and did not know it was so bad. I then again repeated my regrets to the Abbot for not being able to meet the wishes of the Tashi Lama. In this particular case, much to my regret, I was obliged to go against his wishes, but still I hoped that we might yet be friends. I would, however, ask the Abbot to give this advice to His Holiness, that if he wished us to withdraw from Khamba Jong, he should use his influence with the Lhasa authorities to induce them to send proper delegates, and instruct such delegates to discuss matters with us in a reasonable and friendly spirit. Then matters would be very soon settled, and we would return to India. If the Lhasa authorities had done this in the first instance, we might even by now have settled all these frontier matters. The Giaogong lands belonged to the province under the Tashi Lama, and if His Holiness wished ever to get them back for his province, he must induce the Lhasa authorities to entirely change their attitude towards us, and in place of obstinate unfriendliness to show us some sign of a desire to meet us in a reasonable spirit. I then made some personal observations to the Abbot, and he said he had from a boy been brought up in a monastery in a religious way, and was not accustomed to dealing with political matters. I told him I envied him his life of devotion. It was my business to have to wrangle about these small political matters, yet I always admired those who spent their lives in the worship of

God. He asked me if he might come and see me again, and I told him he might come and see me every day and all day; and Captain O'Connor, who could speak Tibetan, would often pay him visits. My aim throughout this interview was to get these Shigatse men to use their influence with the Lhasa authorities to change their present stubborn attitude. I do not hope for much result from this, as the Lhasa influence is too preponderating to be much affected. Still I do not wish to lose a single chance of pressing the Lhasa authorities in however small a way. A further aim I had was to establish good relations with the head of, at any rate, one big monastery in Tibet.

P.S.-22nd August.-The Abbot yesterday paid a visit to the Tibetan delegates, and he to-day informed Captain O'Connor that he had tried to persuade them to abandon their present attitude and negotiate with us here, instead of continuing to press us to withdraw to Giaogong. The Abbot told them that, if they would do this, he was convinced the negotiations would be speedily concluded. Captain Parr also informs that the Abbot really did make this representation to the Lhasa delegates after he had visited me. The Lhasa delegates, however, remained unmoved, and said they had strict orders not to negotiate here.

The Abbot has asked to see me again on the 24th.

Diary kept by Captain W. F. O'Connor during the Tibet Frontier Mission.
(Extract.)

20th August, 1903.—A bright clear morning. Maximum temperature 62.5°; minimum 35.5°.

The sister of one of the Lachung men, who are prisoners at Shigatse, came to Khamba Jong yesterday, and had an interview with Mr. White this morning. The relatives of the two men are naturally in great distress regarding the fate of the captives, and have sent in petitions to Mr. White, begging him to procure their release, and the missionary ladies residing at Lachung have also written to him on the matter. The two men are Kinga-duda and Da-join. The former supports a wife, mother and two sisters; and the latter a wife, four children, an old mother, a small brother, and a sister. No news to-day from round about. A letter arrived from Colonel Brander in the evening to say that he is sending 80 men from Tangu to carry out Mr. White's instructions with regard to the expulsion of the Tibetan guards from Giaogong and Tso-lamo and the capture of live-stock. The representatives from Tashi-Chempo have been asked to call to-morrow at noon.

21st August.—A bright morning. Maximum temperature 76.5°; minimum 39°.

The Te-ling Kusho appeared about 10.30, followed soon after by the Jongpen, who brought the presents from the Tashi-Chempo people. These consisted of some bags of barley, skins of butter, two pieces of silk, and some woollen clothes of the country. I had a talk with the Jongpen and the Te-ling Kusho, who told me generally the objects of the visit of the Tashi-Chempo officials, who apparently have been egged on by the Tsong-du to make a strenuous effort to induce us to withdraw from here either to Giaogong or to some place in the Chumbi valley, which is not within their jurisdiction. About noon the Abbot and his following came into camp and were received in the Durbar tent by Colonel Younghusband and Mr. White. The officials numbered eight in all-the Abbot, his Secretary Ba-du-la, the present and former Jongpens, a monk clerk, and two lay officials.

The Abbot is a stout, pleasant-looking man of some 30 to 35 years of age. He is incarnate Lama of the Ngak-je sub-division of the Tashi-Chempo Monastery, and is reputed clever. He is the senior Abbot under the Penchen Rinpoche, and is in all probability by far the highest ecclesiastic of Tibet who has been interviewed by any British Officer since the time of Turner. His manner was quiet and dignified; he spoke at length during the Durbar, but always in a low and somewhat monotonous tone; and he smiled and appeared gratified by Colonel Younghusband's complimentary messages to His Holiness the Tashi Lama and by any friendly remarks addressed to himself. Very little of interest transpired during the interview, which lasted over an hour. The Abbot explained that, although unused to earthly affairs, he had been deputed by the Penchen Rinpoche to visit the British Commissioners, and to request them as a favour, to return from Tibet either to Giaogong or to Yatung in the Chumbi Valley. He said that His

Holiness had been influenced in the matter by the strong representations made to him from Lhasa that the British were trespassing on soil under his jurisdiction, and that he was responsible for their withdrawal. Upon this the Penchen Rinpoche had deputed an Abbot and three other of his officers as his representatives, and he was in hopes that the British Commissioners would favourably consider his request. His words were repeated with little variation by most of the officers in his suite during the course of the interview. Colonel Younghusband in reply informed the Abbot that he very much regretted that, in this particular instance, he was unable to oblige the Penchen Rinpoche, but that he hoped that the Tashi-Chempo representatives would use their influence with the Lhasa officials to induce them to commence negotiations at Khamba Jong. The Abbot promised to confer with the Lhasa officers on the matter, and after some general conversation the representatives withdrew, Colonel Younghusband promising to convey their wishes to the Viceroy.

About 4 p.m. a heavy rainstorm commenced, which, accompanied by cold gusts of wind, lasted till after nightfall.

22nd August.—Damp cloudy morning. Rain fell during the night, and the rain gange registered .71 inch. Maximum temperature 69.5°; minimum 37.5°.

About 1 o'clock the Kumar and I rode down to pay a visit to the Abbot. He and all the other Shigatse officials are encamped in little black yak-hair tents in a sort of small compound near the foot of the Jong. The Te-ling Kusho received us, and we sat for a few minutes in his tent chatting and drinking buttered tea. He is a most hospitable, good-natured man, and thoroughly appreciates "a well-organised and well-delivered joke." He gave us each a brick of the first-class brick-tea which is drunk by well-to-do men in Tibet. I am trying to secure a good selection of the different classes of brick-tea, which I propose later on to show to our Darjeeling and Duars planters as a guide to the local taste. We then went on to see the Abbot. His tent consists of a sort of small enclosure surrounded by a seven-foot canvas wall and open to all the winds of heaven. Over one end, where he had established himself, is a small canopy, and this is his only shelter. He has a raised seat with a sort of little altar on his right hand, where he has placed his sacred images and the small odds and ends with which Buddhist altars are decorated in Tibet. He sat bareheaded with his right arm also bare. He received us in a very friendly manner, and we sat and chatted with him for half an hour on different subjects. His whole life has been devoted to his religious exercises, and he appears quite ignorant of the world at large,- politics, science, history, and geography all equally beyond his ken. He has never travelled beyond the bounds of the Tashi-Chempo Monastery, except to visit his parents at his birth-place, a small hamlet beyond the Tsangpo. He gave us many interesting details regarding his monastic life. Ba-du-la and the other officials then entered, and we turned to politics.

The Abbot said that, on leaving our camp the day before, he had proceeded straight to the Jong, where he had urged upon the Lhasa officials to commence negotiations with us at Khamba Jong as soon as possible; but had received the invariable reply that no negotiations could take place except at Yatung or on the Giaogong frontier. This was the substance of a long discussion. And the Abbot then again urged his request that we should return to the frontier. We conversed on this matter for some time without getting any further. No arguments were adduced by the Tibetans to support their request, and no attempt was made by them to combat ours. All they could say was—"Please go back; we shall get into trouble if you don't." And they also averred that our presence here was raising suspicions in the minds of the Tibetans, which were growing day by day. At the close of the visit Ba–du–la said that a report had reached him from Giaogong that some of his yaks had been captured there by our soldiers, and that his yak-herds had been ill-treated. I promised to enquire into the matter, and we came away.

A heavy rainstorm began about 3 p.m. and lasted for about an hour.

23rd August.—There was some rain during the night, .14 inch registered. Maximum temperature 56.5° : minimum 38.5°.

The Te–ling Kusho called on the Kumar, and I had a very interesting conversation with him in the evening. He gave us a number of details regarding the great Ne-chung oracle at Lhasa, which appears to carry no small weight in the political concerns of this most extraordinary Government. The oracle (the "Ne-chung-chö-je") is a man selected by certain tests in childhood. When required to prophecy, a regular formal ceremony is gone through. The oracle is seated upon a golden throne, incense is burned, and a number of monks, seated in a semi-circle, chant and play. After some little time a violent trembling fit seizes the oracle, and he rocks himself wildly to-and-fro. This is the sign that the "God has entered his belly," as the Tibetans say, and a huge golden helmet, of immense weight and garnished with all kinds of precious stones, is immediately placed upon his head and securely fastened below his chin. Questions are now put to him, generally by a Shape, regarding future events, such as the prospects of peace or war, and the appointment of high officials, and the answers are written down. After this the oracle rises and dances for a while to the sound of the monks' music, when he suddenly falls lifeless upon the ground. The great hat is now removed with all speed and the oracle revives. The hat is said to weigh several maunds, and its weight could not possibly be endured except by a being inspired with divine strength.

[Any one who has ever seen one of the "Bitans" of witch-women of the Gilgit district go through their performances, will be astonished at the resemblance between the ceremonies, conducted with similar aim, in countries so different and so far apart.]

There is no news from the country round about

except that all the roads are being very closely watched.

Letter from Colonel F. E. Younghusband, C.I.E., British Commissioner, Tibet Frontier Commission, to the Secretary to the Government of India, in the Foreign Department, dated Khamba Jong, the 24th August, 1903.

I have the honour to report that the Abbot deputed by the Tashi Lama of Tashi Lampo called upon me again to-day, and after lunching in the Commission mess adjourned to my tent, where another conversation of two hours' duration took place.

He informed me that, after his last visit, he had gone to the Lhasa representatives, and urged them to negotiate here instead of continuing to press for the negotiation to take place at Giaogong. But they had replied that just as my orders were to negotiate here, theirs were to negotiate at Giaogong, so they could not agree to anything different.

The Abbot, therefore, now came to say that there were several hundred Tibetan troops near here, but he would get those withdrawn if I would send away my escort. He thought that then probably the Lhasa Government would consent to negotiations here. I told him that I had not the slightest objection to the presence of the Tibetan troops; and when they had so many hundreds near, it surprised me that they should have any objection to the small number of only two hundred which I had.

The Abbot then asked, if I would not send the

whole away, would I send one hundred away, and he would himself remain with us as a hostage that no harm would fall us. He explained that the Tibetans thought we had not come with friendly intent, as we had forced our way into the country, and a reduction of our escort would appease them. I told the Abbot I could not acknowledge that we had forced our way into Tibet. On the contrary, I had up till now ignored the presence of Tibetan soldiers inside the Treaty frontier who had no business to be where they were. As to the strength of my escort, I said that he was unacquainted with the custom of big countries; that we had not taken any objection to the Amban taking a very much larger escort down to India; and it seemed to me great impoliteness on their part to make these frequent objections to the strength of my escort. An escort was as much the appendage of an officer of high rank employed on important duty in a foreign country as were his headdress and his sword. The presence of an escort did not necessarily imply an unfriendly intent, and in a great country like this 200 men are altogether too small a number for hostile purposes. I thanked him for volunteering to go hostage for me, but said I had no fear in the matter. I had travelled for many thousands of miles in the Chinese Empire absolutely alone; and if I were here on private business, I would have no hesitation in coming alone here, too, without a single soldier. But as I was here now on important official business, the Viceroy would, I was sure, be very angry if I consented to abrogate any of the dignity due to my high rank.

The Abbot very politely apologised for all the trouble he was giving me by making so many requests, and said his only object was to find some way by which negotiations could be commenced and the present trouble to the Tashi Lama avoided. I told him he might make requests to me all day long, and he would always find me ready to listen to him and to give him what I, at any rate, considered reasonable answers. I much regretted the inconvenience being caused to the Tashi Lama, and I felt sure that, if the conduct of these negotiations rested with His Holiness and the polite and reasonable advisers of his whom he had sent to me, we should very soon come to a settlement. My advice was to again represent to the Lhasa representatives the trouble which the Lhasa Government were causing to His Holiness; and to get His Holiness also to represent matters directly at Lhasa.

The Abbot replied that they were not allowed to make representation against the orders of the Lhasa Government. Nevertheless, he would again this very day go to the Lhasa delegates; tell them how he had once more tried to induce me to go back to Giagong; then to send my escort back; and then to send half my escort; and how I had refused all these requests. He would then ask them to make a request to Lhasa to open negotiations here. The Abbot added that he would even go so far as to tell them he would under-take to receive in their stead any punishment which the Lhasa Government might order upon the dele-gates for daring to make this request.

He then asked me what we wanted in the coming negotiations. I told him that I had set this forth fully in a speech I had made on my first arrival here, a copy of which I would be very glad to give him. He was, however, acquainted with it, and asked me what was meant exactly by opening a trade route. I explained that we wanted a proper trade mart which would not be closed with a wall behind it as Yatung had been-a mart where Indian traders could come and meet Tibetan traders-a mart such as we had in other parts of the Chinese Empire, and had formerly had at Shigatse itself. "When that is open," I said, "you will be able to buy all your things much cheaper than you can now." He laughed heartily at this, for he is a genial, hearty man. Curiously enough they also laughed equally heartily when I said that the new treaty would have to be much stricter than the old one, for they had continued to break the old one year after year, and we should, of course, therefore, have to be strict with them to see that they did not break the new. They are very like big children, and said "If we were not able to keep the old one, how can we be expected to keep one still more strict."

They left promising to talk the matter over with the Lhasa officials, and asking to be allowed to come and see me again.

Letter from Colonel F. E. Younghusband, C.I.E., British Commissioner, Tibet Frontier Commission, to the Secretary to the Government of India, in the Foreign Department, dated Khamba Jong, the 27th August, 1903.

In continuation of my letter, dated the 20th August, 1903, I have the honour to forward, for the information of the Government of India, a copy of further correspondence which has taken place between me and Mr. Ho, regarding the removal of Tibetans from the Sikkim side of the frontier.

I have been informed by Lieutenant-Colonel Brander that the Tibetans have been removed from the posts they were occupying, and a small blockhouse they had erected near Giaogong was destroyed.

About 200 yaks and 50 sheep were also seized.

The Abbot from Shigatse in his interview with me on the 24th instant represented to me that many of these yaks and sheep belonged to the Tashi Lama, and asked me to release them. I explained to him that we had been obliged to seize these animals, as two Lachung men had been seized and beaten; and in spite of repeated requests, the Lhasa officials would give us no information about them, nor deliver them up.

The Abbot assured me that they had been seized by orders of the Lhasa Government, and the Tashi Lama had nothing whatever to do with the seizure, and he would state this in writing under his seal, if necessary.

I replied that this was, then, one more instance of the trouble the Lhasa authorities were bringing the Shigatse people into by their unfriendly attitude towards the Commission. I could not, of course, recognise any difference between Shigatse and Lhasa, and had to look to the Tibetan Government as a whole; but I would advise him to induce the Lhasa officials to pay without delay the sum of Rs. 2,000 which Mr. White had demanded from them as indemnity for the ill-usage to the two Lachung men, and to deliver them up as soon as possible. When that was done, the animals seized would be at once released.

Annexure 1.

Letter from Colonel F. E. Younghusband, C.I.E., British Commissioner, Tibet Frontier Commission, to Mr. Ho Kuang-hsieh, dated Khamba Jong, the 19th August, 1903.

It having come to my notice that Tibetans are occupying positions at Giaogong, Tso Lama, and Lonakh, all situated on streams which flow into the Teesta, and therefore in territory, which, according to the Convention of 1890, belongs to the British Protected State of Sikkim, I have the honour to request that you will procure their withdrawal with the least possible delay.

Annexure 2.

Letter from Mr. Ho Kuang-hsieh, to Colonel F. E. Younghusband, C.I.E., British Commissioner. Tibet Frontier Commission, dated Khamba Jong, the 20th August, 1903.

I have the honour to acknowledge the receipt yesterday of your letter of the same date, together with translation of original which was handed to the

Tibetan officers, and, in reply, beg to inform you that, as a result of my enquiries concerning Giaogong and the other places referred to in your letter, I find that no troops have been recently despatched there, but that, for some time past, some 20 Hsunting have been stationed at these places.

The long-standing trouble with the Tibetans originated in their refusal to recognise the boundary as laid down in the Convention of 1890, but as you have come to discuss this question, and the boundary line has not up to the present been definitely settled, I hope that, if the matter is not of paramount importance, Giaogong will not be closed to these men before the question is finally settled. I beg, therefore, that you will in the meanwhile overlook their presence, and subsequently, when the question has been fully discussed, the matter can then be adjusted. As you are fully cognisant of the Tibetans' feelings, you will not, I trust, misunderstand my meaning.
Annexure 3.

Letter from Colonel F. E. Younghusband, C.I.E., British Commissioner, Tibet Frontier Commission, to Mr. Ho Kuang-hsieh, dated Khamba Jong, the 22nd August, 1903.

I have the honour to acknowledge the receipt of your letter, dated 20th August, and in reply to say that I had up till now overlooked the presence of a few Tibetans who were stationed inside the boundary line laid down by the Convention of 1890. But as I had been informed that the number of these Tibetans was increasing, and as the more I have become cognisant of the feelings of the Tibetans, as represented by the Lhasa Government, the more unfriendly they have appeared to me, I have had no resource left but to demand from you their withdrawal, and to take measures to see that they should withdraw.

If the Lhasa Government had shown a more friendly spirit towards this Commission, I would have had much pleasure in complying with your request, and to have continued to have overlooked the presence of these Tibetans inside the boundary laid down by the treaty. Under existing circumstances, I regret I am unable to meet your wishes, but must proceed to enforce our treaty rights in respect to the boundary. Annexure 4.

Letter from Mr. Ho Kuang-hsieh and Captain Parr, to Colonel F. E. Younghusband, C.I.E., British Commissioner, Tibet Frontier Commission, dated Khamba Jong, the 24th August, 1903.

I have the honour to acknowledge the receipt yesterday of your second letter, &c.

The object of coming here was to discuss frontier and trade matters, but if before any discussion has taken place friendly relations are imperilled by the expulsion across the frontier of those Hsunting whose presence there was of minor importance, subsequent negotiations will be most difficult. We have explained matters fully to the Tibetan officers, and beg that you will kindly consult with Mr. White, so as to allow the

question of the expulsion of the Tibetans across frontier to remain in abeyance for the present, and for which consideration we will be most grateful.
Annexure 5.

Letter from Colonel F. E. Younghusband, C.I.E., British Commissioner, Tibet Frontier Commission, to Mr. Ho Kuang-hsieh and Captain Parr, dated kamba Jong, the 25th August, 1903.

I have the honour to acknowledge the receipt of your letter of yesterday's date. I note that you consider the matter as one of minor importance-a point of view from which I differ entirely. My orders for the expulsion of the Tibetan soldiers have already been issued, and I must decline to discuss this matter any further.

Diary kept by Captain W. F. O'Connor during the Tibet Frontier Mission.
(Extract.)

24th August, 1903.—Still cloudy, but some blue sky showing. .1 inch rain registered. Maximum temperature 63.5°; minimum 41.5°.

The Abbot having expressed a wish to call upon Colonel Younghusband again, an invitation was sent to him and Ba-du-la to come and lunch with us and discuss matters afterwards. At one o'clock accordingly these two arrived in camp and sat for a few minutes in the Kumar's tent, where we showed the Abbot the celestial and terrestrial globes. He was especially interested in the former, wherein he recognised all the twelve signs of the Zodiac, calling them by the same names that we use; and he gave us an interesting little lecture on the science of astronomy as known in Tibet. Tibetan astronomy comes from the Hindus, and consists mainly of a mass of absurd superstitions and legends grafted upon very accurate observations of the actual movements of the heavenly bodies. The Abbot seemed to enjoy his luncheon, although he would not, of course, touch wine or tobacco. He partook of curry, fruit, and other dishes, and drank tea made in the European fashion, but without sugar. After tiffin he was joined by his steward or Di-chung-wa and the Khamba Jongpen, and these four had an interview with the two Commissioners. They began by explaining that on leaving our camp after the last interview, they had proceeded straight to the Jong, and had endeavoured to persuade the two Lhasa officials to commence negotiations here, but had failed to do so, and so had come to visit us again with the hope of persuading us to do one of three things,–either to return to the frontier, or to send away our escort, or, if we could not do this, at any rate to reduce the escort. Colonel Younghusband declined very naturally to do any of these things, and clearly explained his reasons. They then tried to sound the Commissioners as to what would be the basis of the new treaty which we were proposing to negotiate, and in especial what we meant by a tsong-lam, or trade-route. Colonel Younghusband explained that a "trade-route," as we intended it, meant increased facilities for traders, and that, as regards the new treaty, it would certainly be of a stricter nature than the last one. This seemed to amuse them, for they laughed and said-"If the Tibetans wouldn't observe the old treaty, it wasn't likely that they would observe a stricter one." It did not seem to occur to them that it may be possible to compel observance of treaty rights. Ba-du-la then said that he had heard that our soldiers from Tangu had captured certain cattle belonging some to the Penchen Rinpoche and some to his peasants. It was explained to him that these cattle had been seized as an indemnity for the capture of the two Lachung men at Shigatse, and that on on payment of Rs. 2,000 they would be released. They protested that the Tsang people were in no way responsible for the seizure of the two men, to which Colonel Younghusband replied that in that case the best course they could adopt was to refer to the Lhasa officials on the question, for we were unable to distinguish in such matters between the Supreme and Local Governments of Tibet, and besides, the unfriendly attitude assumed by the Lhasa Government was constantly getting the Tsang people into trouble. They said that they would at once approach the Lhasa officials on the matter. Colonel Younghusband then informed them that he would be pleased to receive them and hear what they had to say whenever they chose to pay him a visit, and with this the interview concluded. The Abbot then came and had some tea in my tent. I showed him Dr. Waddell's book on Lamaism, with which he was delighted, and with which we presented him.

A letter came from Captain Cooke of the 32nd Pioneers to inform Colonel Younghusband that he had destroyed the block-house at Tso-lamo, and seized upon some 200 yaks and 30 sheep.

25th August.—Cloudy morning. Maximum temperature 63.5°; minimum 40.5°.

Spent morning in camp reading and writing. In the afternoon Mr. White and I rode up a nulla lying westwards some 4 or 5 miles from here, and shot 21 hares in a couple of hours. A convoy arrived, bringing in the Swiss Cottage tent which we are proposing to use as a mess tent instead of Mr. White's tent which we are using at present for that purpose; but as one of the poles and all the kanats have been left behind, it is useless at present.

26th August.—Still cloudy. Maximum temperature 64°; minimum 39.5°.

A very disagreeable day-cold wind blowing continuously. Captain Parr called in the afternoon. The Tibetans-both Lhasa and Tashi-Chempo representatives-are to call upon the Commissioners officially to-morrow at 2 P.M. There is no news from round about.

From the Foreign Secretary, Simla, to Colonel F. E. Younghusband, C.I.E., Khamba Jong viâ Tele-camp (Sikkim), dated the 7th September, 1903.
(Telegraphic.)

With reference to protest by Lhasa and Tashi officials, regarding our presence at Khamba Jong, please inform them and Chinese Commissioners of intimation conveyed by Prince Ching on 19th July to Chargé d'Affaires at Peking that Amban had written that Dalai Lama, on hearing of despatch of British and Chinese Commissioners to Khamba Jong, had replied: "That it is his duty, the matter being a very important one, also to appoint interpreter officials above the usual rank to proceed with proper credentials to Khamba and in company with the Prefect Shou to meet the British delegates and discuss the frontier question with them." In the face of this reply of the Dalai Lama, the objections now raised by the Tibetan officers to our presence at Khamba Jong appear to be unwarranted.

Letter from Lieutenant-Colonel C. W. Ravenshaw, Officiating Resident in Nepal, to the Secretary to the Government of India, in the Foreign Department, dated the Residency, Nepal, the 4th September, 1903.

I enclose, for the information of the Government of India, a translation of a letter from the Prime Minister of Nepal to the Honourable the four Kazis of Lhasa, which the Prime Minister has sent me, and writes that it has been despatched.

P.S.-I am sending a copy to Colonel Younghusband.

Annexure.

Letter from His Excellency Maharaja Chandra Shamsher Jang, Rana Bahadur, Thong-Lin-Pimma, Kokang Wang-Syan, Prime Minister and Marshal of Nepal, to the Honourable the four Kazis of Lhasa, dated Samvat, 1960. (Translation.)

After compliments.-Here all well, hope same there. From information received from my officials at the frontier and also from various newspaper reports, it appears that the Commissioners deputed by the British Government to see to the enforcement of the terms of the Anglo-Tibetan Conventions of 1890 and 1893, which had not been observed and carried into effect by the Tibetan Government, have been staying at a place called Khamba Jong, and that in the absence of fully empowered Commissioners from Tibet to deal with the matters in dispute, and owing to the indifference of the local officials of the place no settlement could be arrived at, and the British Commissioners are being unnecessarily detained there. But your complete silence on this subject makes me anxious. The friendly and fraternal relations of long standing between the Nepal and the Tibetan Governments induce me on the present occasion to enlighten you with my views concerning this matter, which I am confident will prove beneficial to you (if acted on).

Some time ago I had an occasion to enquire of you in my letter of Bhadra Badi 8th, Friday, Samvat, 1958, whether there was any truth in the rumours that were current regarding certain secret arrangements being made between your Government and that of Russia, when I received a reassuring reply, dated Marga Sudi 5th, Monday, Samvat, 1958, to the effect that the rumours had no foundation in truth, and that they were being circulated in the newspapers with a view to bring about a rupture between the Governments of Nepal and Tibet, and this reassurance, coupled with the conviction that such revolutionary steps could never be taken by men of your intelligence, led me to allow our friendly relations to continue as before.

Now again, although it is long since the British Commissioners arrived at Khamba Jong with a view to discuss and bring about a settlement satisfactory to both parties of all matters relating to the aforesaid Convention, yet your omission to depute any Commissioners vested with full authority, and your neglect or failure to bring about a reasonable settlement so long, compel me to think that such unjustifiable conduct on your part might lead to grave consequences and fill my mind with serious misgivings.

It is laid down in the treaty concluded on Chaitra Badi 3rd, Monday, Samvat, 1912, between the Governments of Nepal and Tibet that this Government will assist Tibet in case of an invasion of its territory by any foreign Rajas. Consequently, when a difference of opinion arises between you and any one else, it is incumbent on me to help you to the best of my power with my advice and guidance in order to prevent any troubles befalling you from such difference, and the manner in which you have managed this business not appearing commendable, the assistance to be rendered to you by me at this crisis of your own creation, consists in giving you such advice as will conduce to the welfare of your country. The said advice is given below, and I am fully confident that you will, after due deliberation, lay it before the Potala Lama and come to a speedy conclusion to act according to it. Should you fail to follow my advice and trouble befall you, there would be no way open to me to assist you in any other way in the troublous situation brought about by you without listening to my advice and following a wayward course of your own. Understand it well; for the British Government does not appear to have acted in an improper or high-handed manner in this matter, but is simply trying to have the conditions of the treaty fulfilled, to which everybody has a right, and it is against the treaty, as well as against all morality or policy, to allow matters to drift and to regard as enemies the officers of such a powerful Government who have come to enforce such rights. Besides, when His Majesty the Emperor of China has, for your good, posted Ambans of high rank, it is a serious mistake on your part to disregard even their advice, and neglect to carry on business with the British Commissioners.

Advice.

(1.) You are fully aware of the greatness of the British power. It is against all policy to disparage and to behave as if you had no concern with the Commissioners deputed by such a powerful

Government to discuss the terms of the treaty concluded between the two Governments.

(2.) It is the bounden duty of every one to abide by a treaty made by oneself. It will be a serious failure of duty on your part if a calamity befalls your country through your not acting in a straightforward and reasonable manner with the powerful British Government which is actuated simply by such lawful motives.

(3.) It is said that you refuse to be bound by the Anglo-Tibetan Treaty of 1890 on the ground that it was not concluded by you, but by the Chinese. If this report is correct, then you have acted very improperly. You and we have for a long time held in high respect His Majesty the Emperor of China, as is quite clear from the wording of the Treaty of 1912 between Nepal and Tibet. It is improper to declare that the aforesaid Convention, having been made by the Chinese, is not binding upon you, since whatever was done was done on your behalf. It is against reason for you to say so.

(4.) I may point out here that, since the conclusion of the Treaty of Samvat, 1872, between the British and the Nepal Governments, representatives of both the Governments have resided in the two countries, and the due observance of the terms of the treaty has been continually advantageous to the Government of Nepal, nor has my religion suffered in any way. The advantages derived from such arrangement are too many to enumerate. Since the treaty was made, the British Government has on different occasions restored to us territories lost by Nepal in war and producing a revenue of many lakhs of rupees. This fact should also be known to you.

(5.) You must bear in mind that the Government you are to deal with are not a despotic, but a constitutional one, and this will be corroborated by the fact that they have helped us to maintain the autonomy of our country up to so long a time, whereas they might have easily deprived us of it if they had a mind to behave with us in a despotic and unjust manner. The most notable feature in our relation with the British Government is that they sacredly observed our religious and social prejudices. Hence if you can even now take time by the forelock to settle the hanging questions and behave with them as your true friends hereafter, I am sure Tibet will derive the same benefit from such alliance as Nepal has hitherto done. I need not mention here how happy I should be if your relations with the British Government were as cordial as those of mine.

(6.) That the British Government have any evil designs upon Tibet does not appear from any source. it is well known that the sun never sets upon the British dominions. That the Sovereign of such a vast Empire entertains designs of unjustly and improperly taking your mountainous country should never cross your mind.

(7.) Tibet is a great home of Budhism. There should not be the least suspicion of the English meddling with that religion, for it is not their rule to interfere with other people's religion. On the contrary, their interest for Budhism is apparent from the fact that, after consulting old religious books, they fixed upon the site of Kapilavastu, the birth-place of Budha, as being situated in the Butwal district of Nepal, and when upon the strength of this information we traced the place and dug it up, foundations of old buildings were discovered, and we found out also the ancient image of Budha with his mother situated in the Lummini Garden.

(8.) Thinking that to bring about unnecessary complications with the British Government is like producing headache by twisting a rope round one's head when it is not aching. I have written to you my views, and I see it clearly that, if you disregard my advice, a serious calamity is likely to overtake you.

(9.) I am in hopes that I shall soon have reassuring news of you.

From Colonel F. E. Younghusband, C.I.E., Khamba Jong, to the Foreign Secretary, Simla, dated the 8th September, 1903.
(Telegraphic.)

Your telegram 2nd September. Offer of yaks quite invaluable. Five hundred in a month's time would be most acceptable.

From Colonel F. E. Younghusband, C.I.E., Khamba Jong, to the Foreign Secretary, Simla, dated Khamba Jong, the 9th (despatched from Telegraph Camp, Sikkim, on 10th) September, 1903.
(Telegraphic.)

Your telegram of 2nd instant. I have written recommending, besides movement of twenty-third Pioneers to Jalap-la route, the increase of my escort by one hundred men from the supports, and the acceptance from Nepal of five hundred yaks. All these moves to take place in about a month's time. If hostilities are forced on us, I recommend occupation of Chumbi Valley to be followed by advance of the Mission to Gyantse.

∞◌◐◑◌∞

Political Diary of the Tibet Frontier Commission.
(Extract.)

31st August, 1903.—A trustworthy informant visited
me in the morning and spoke in rather a serious way
of the present situation. He says, from a number of
small indications, he is convinced that the Tibetans
will do nothing till they are made to-till a situation
has been produced and they have been compelled to
come to terms. They are quite sure in their own

minds that they are fully equal to us; and far from our getting anything out of them, they think that they will be able to force something out of us. Some 2,600 Tibetan soldiers are believed, he says, to be occupying the heights and passes along a line running between Phari and Shigatse. 1,000 rifles manufactured at Lhasa have been issued to the Lhasa Command, and 500 each to the Phari and Shigatse Commands. He does not think, however, that they will attack us for the present, though they may in the winter, when they think our communication is cut off by snow. Their present policy is one of passive obstruction. They have made up their minds to have no negotiations with us inside Tibet; and they will simply leave us here; while, if we try to advance further, they will oppose us by force. They are afraid that, if they give us an inch we will take an ell; and if they allow us here one year, we will go to Shigatse the next and Lhasa the next. So they are determined to stop us at the start.

At the same time these Lhasa delegates-and the local officials, to curry favour, encourage them in the view-are very indisposed towards us. They say we give them a great deal of trouble here; and the Depon (General) has gone so far as to say (to his own people) that he does not like meat as a rule, but he would not at all mind eating our flesh.

The Shigatse Abbot has done his best to make the Lhasa officials take a more reasonable view, but without success. And the Lhasa officials are entirely ruled by the National Assembly at Lhasa, chiefly composed of Lhasa monks.

A report is current that we wish to open shops at Lhasa, Shigatse, and Gyantse; and the Depon gives out that, if we want to do this, we shall have to do it by force, for the Tibetans would never agree to it. I told the trustworthy informant that we had formerly had a mart at Shigatse; that business had been carried on there for years without trouble; and I could not see why there should be trouble if we had a mart there again.

1st September.—Mr. Ho paid me an official visit to-day to say he had been recalled to Lhasa on account of ill-health. Previous to his visit he had also written me a letter to the same effect. I told him I was sorry I should lose the pleasure of his company for some time, but I hoped he would take advantage of his journey to Lhasa to advance the business we had in hand by explaining to the Amban the position of affairs here. "It did not seem to me," I said, "that the Amban at all realised in how serious a light we regarded the present negotiations; nor the responsibility which rested upon the Chinese in regard to them." I then recounted how, under the Chifoo Convention of 1876 we had become entitled to receive passports; how in 1885 passports for such a mission were given to Mr. Macaulay; how, in deference to the subsequently expressed wishes of the Chinese, we had countermanded that mission; how this regard for the wishes had only resulted in the Tibetans invading the territory of a British Feudatory; how, again, in consideration for the

Chinese, we had refrained for nearly two years from taking any action against the Tibetans, in the hope that the Chinese would exercise their authority over them; how, being disappointed in our expectations, we had been obliged to turn them out of Sikkim and pursue them into Chumbi; how, even there, again in deference to the wishes of the Chinese, we had abstained from re-occupying the Chumbi Valley; how the Amban had come down to Sikkim to settle affairs between us and the Tibetans, assuming all responsibility for them, engaging to obtain the formal assent of the Lhasa Government to any agreement he might make with us, but professing to treat this as a matter of little importance; how we had concluded a treaty with the Amban; and, lastly, how the Tibetans had systematically broken and repudiated that treaty, while the Chinese professed their incapacity to hold them to it.

All this, I said, made a very serious position. The British Government had time after time shown consideration to the Chinese Government, but the net result was that the Tibetans had broken the old treaty and now placed every obstacle in the way of negotiating a new one.

The only reply which Mr. Ho made to this was that the Tibetans were a difficult people to deal with; that they took exception to many parts of the treaty which the Amban had made on their behalf, and this was the reason why they would not observe it.

The Shigatse Abbot and some other Tibetans-though not the Lhasa delegates-had accompanied Mr.

Ho; and he, after explaining the situation to them, said to me that the Tibetans objected to negotiating at Khamba Jong, and asked me myself to tell them our decision to remain here was final. I said I had already told them so a hundred times; but that it was his business more than mine; and that I must trust to him to represent this matter to the Amban, and impress upon him the importance of using his influence with the Tibetan Government to make them change their present attitude. Not only Mr. Ho himself, but also the Amban, had written to say that, if the Viceroy did not care for negotiations to take place at Yatung, he was quite prepared to conduct them at any other place which the Viceroy might select. Seeing that we had a right to send a mission to Lhasa, and seeing that the last negotiations were conducted at Calcutta, His Excellency might very reasonably have selected Lhasa as the place for the present negotiations. And when he selected Khamba Jong, there could be no possible justification for objecting to it.

This the Amban must impress upon the Lhasa Government, who did not seem to understand that for years they had been offending the British Government, and whom it ill became, therefore, to object to the mere place where negotiations should be held. We had given them the opportunity of negotiating, and if the Lhasa Government still persisted in refusing to hold negotiations here, and the Chinese still showed their incapacity to make them negotiate at this place, the Amban must understand, I said, that the position would become very grave indeed, and

the Chinese and Tibetans would only have themselves to thank if, under those circumstances, the
British Government took matters into their own
hands and adopted their own measures for effecting a
settlement.

Mr. Ho said he would explain this to the Amban
and he also then explained it to the Tibetans present,
who seemed to a certain extent impressed, though
they said that we were acting in a very oppressive
manner.

The conversation then turned on the question of
our seizure of the yaks. The Abbot said the animals
would suffer from being confined, and he asked when
they would be released. I told him that they were
allowed to graze every day, and that, if he thought
they were suffering, their immediate release could be
procured by bringing the two men who had been
seized and beaten, and by paying the sum of Rs. 2,000
we demand as compensation for their ill-treatment.

I then told Mr. Ho that this was another case
which he should represent to the Amban, for it, too,
was becoming serious. Two British-protected subjects
had been without cause seized and beaten by the
Tibetans. It had been contended that the men had no
right to be at Shigatse; but even if they had no right
there, the Tibetans had no right to seize and beat
them. We did not, however, acknowledge that the
Lachung men had no right. On the contrary, it had
long been their custom to trade with Shigatse. I added
that even British Indian subjects used to trade there,
and have had a regular mart there for many years.

Mr. Ho promised to represent all that I had said during this interview to the Amban, and he was confident some action would be taken.

The Tibetans throughout made repeated assertions that the Lhasa delegates would not negotiate here; and the absence of the delegates on this occasion, and still more their refusal to accompany Mr. Ho on a visit last week which he had actually arranged to make me, and which he had to abandon at the last moment on account of their refusal, is sufficient proof, both of their determination not to discuss matters here, and of the incompetence of the Chinese representative to make them act in accordance with his wishes.

The Tibetans also asked that I would forward to the Viceroy their request to have negotiations conducted elsewhere. I informed them that I had not yet heard from them any sufficient reason which I could submit to His Excellency as justification for a reconsideration of the matter.

2nd September–I had arranged to return Mr. Ho's visit this afternoon; but early this morning I received a letter from Captain Parr, saying that after yesterday's interview Mr. Ho had decided to leave for Lhasa early this morning. Mr. Ho asked him to convey to me "his appreciation of my extreme courtesy and consideration throughout his sojourn here." Captain Parr added that Mr. Ho "seemed sanguine that his efforts to induce a more enlightened policy at Lhasa would not be barren of results"; and he had assured Captain Parr that he would not fail to place the views expressed by me at yesterday's interview before the Amban and the Tibetan Council.

I wrote a private note to Captain Parr in reply, asking him to express my regrets to Mr. Ho that I had not been able to have the pleasure of returning his visit, and to tell him that every word I said yesterday was well-weighed and considered beforehand, and not one word was said which was not meant in earnest. I trusted, therefore, that if he wished to save this country from trouble, he would impress most earnestly upon the Amban the necessity of taking action before it was too late.

That Mr. Ho will be able to effect much is, however, doubtful. He is not a man of any strength of character, for if he was, he would have been able to assert himself much more forcibly over his Tibetan colleagues than he has done. Moreover, the Chinese Government itself is evidently very lukewarm over this business, and he is not the man to run against the general current. There is even, too, a rumour which has reached Mr. Wilton that he is being recalled in disgrace, which would make it still less likely that he would be able to exert any influence at Lhasa.

F. E. YOUNGHUSBAND,
British Commissioner.
Khamba Jong,
The 2nd September, 1903.

∘⟨⟨✕⟩⟩∘

Diary Kept by Captain W. F. O'Connor during the Tibet Frontier Mission
(Extract.)

27th August, 1903.—A cloudy morning. Maximum temperature 67.9°; minimum 38.5°.

The Tibetan officers who were to have visited us this morning sent an excuse by Captain Parr to say that they would rather not come. The reason assigned to Captain Parr was that they were in doubt as to the manner in which they were likely to be received; but it is probable that this is a mere subterfuge, and that in reality they are unwilling to commit themselves in any way whatever. At any rate, the proposed interview fell through.

A convoy arrived in the afternoon bringing some tents, mess stores, &c.

Large stores of fodder and fuel continue to arrive daily at the Jong.

28th August.—Still cloudy. Maximum temperature 66.5°; minimum 37°.

An uneventful day. Towards evening the sky cleared and the snows stood out plainly all around. There seems every prospect of a complete change for the better in the weather.

Note from a trustworthy informant. It is rumoured that the Tibetan garrison between here and Shigatse has been largely reinforced. The estimated strength of the Shigatse, Gyantse, and Phari Commands is 2,600 men. Two thousand of the new rifles are said to have been distributed: 1,000 to the Lhasa garrison, and 500 each to the Shigatse and Phari garrisons.

29th August.—This is the finest morning we have had for some weeks. There are still scattered cumulus clouds in the sky, but the snows of the Sikkim frontier are quite clear, and the air is fresh and exhilarating. Maximum temperature 70.5°; minimum 35°.

We took some photographs during the morning, including a group of one member of each of the different tribes and nations represented in our camp. It included a Tibetan, a Chinaman, a Sikkim Bhutia, a Sherpa Bhutia (from Eastern Nepal), a Lepcha, a Bhutanese, a Nepali, a Punjabi Sikh, a Hindu, a Mussulman, and two half-Tibetan half-Chinese "braves" from Captain Parr's escort. Lieutenant Bailey took a patrol out beyond Lung-dong village in the morning, and found nothing but six Tibetan soldiers in the village. In the afternoon Mr. White and I and the Kumar rode out eastwards and shot some hares. It is said now that the Tibetans will refuse to allow the Sikkim men who have sheep grazing in Tibet to drive their sheep back to Sikkim-that they will, in fact, confiscate them; this, of course, as a counterblast to our action in seizing their sheep and yaks in Giaogong. They have definitely refused to allow the Lachung people to bring in their flocks of sheep without permission of the Jongpen. This permission is now being asked, and it remains to be seen what the answer will be.

30th August.—A fine bright morning. Maximum temperature 68.5°; minimum 35°.

Colonel Younghusband and Mr. Bailey rode up the Khamba Jong nulla, and secured six species of birds, some frogs, &c., to add to the stock of specimens of Tibetan fauna. About 2 p.m. a thunderstorm ushered in a heavy hail and rainstorm. This was quite the heaviest shower we have had, and in a few minutes a stream of water found its way into camp by the main entrance and effectually drenched a large number of tents. The shower only lasted about half an hour, but .44 inches was registered in the rain gauge. It was interesting to notice that the thermometer went down 36° (from 72° to 36°) at a run when the shower began.

It appears that the Jongpen has given permission to the Lachung headman to take a way his sheep into Sikkim if he wishes to do so.

Mr. White and Mr. Wilton rode some four to five miles up the Khamba Jong nulla, and crossing the hills to the north, descended into the Yaru Chu valley and rode home via Se-kang village and the Kozo hot springs. They escaped the thunderstorm which seems to have been very local in its range.

31st August.—Light rain lasting from 4.30 a.m. to about 8 a.m. Total rainfall registered during 24 hours .46 inches. A dark cloudy morning. Maximum temperature 70.2°; minimum 41°.
Average maximum temperature during the month 68.23°

,, minimum ,, ,, ,,38.9°
Highest maximum ,, ,, ,,76.5°
Lowest minimum ,, ,, ,,35.0°
Total rainfall registered during the month 2.61″
The statistics for July (11th to 31st) were-
Average maximum temperature 69.65°
,, minimum temperature 38.89°

Highest maximum ,,75.8°
Lowest minimum ,,35.0°
Total rainfall registered 0.122″
(Some light rain fell before the arrival of the rain guage).

A Tibetan returned from Rhe reports that there are no Tibetan soldiers at Rhe, but that he hears there are 200 at Yago a little further on. Ho and the Tashi-Chempo Abbot are to call on our camp at 12 noon to-morrow.

1st September. Another dark cloudy morning. Light rain during the night. .022 registered. Maximum temperature 65.9°; minimum 37.9°.

At noon Mr. Ho, the Abbot, and Ba-du-la called on the Commissioners. During the ensuing interview Colonel Younghusband impressed upon Mr. Ho the serious nature of the course of obstruction now being pursued by the Tibetans, and begged him to explain this aspect of the case both to the present and the coming Ambans. This Mr. Ho promised to do. The Tashi-Chempo officials then put forward their threadbare requests on the old lines, raising the question of our presence here and the impossibility of any negotiations being conducted at Khamba Jong, and begging for the return of the livestock which we had seized at Giaogong. To this Colonel Younghusband gave a firm and uncompromising answer to the effect that we have no intention of moving from here, and as regards the animals, they must endeavour to settle that question with the Lhasa representatives, and that, on the production of our two Sikkim men and of Rs. 1,000 each as compensation, the animals would be restored. Mr. Ho also communicated this reply to the Tibetans, and the interview closed.

I hear from the Te-ling Kusho that the Jongpen has just had news of his father's death and is at present in mourning. Tibetan mourning lasts for 49 days. All ornaments are removed, and for three days the mourners do not leave the house. After the three days they may leave the house, but they do not resume their ornaments or wash their faces until the expiration of the 49 days. The funeral obsequies are of an extraordinary and, to our ideas, barbarous nature.

A trustworthy informant tells me that he hears the rifles of native manufacture are of the gas-pipe order, and that several have burst at practice; and also that the ammunition is of a very inferior kind. They are of the Martini pattern.

The Chinese officer, who is to act here during Ho's absence, has arrived at Khamba from Chumbi.

2nd September.—A cloudy morning. .012 rain yesterday. Maximum temperature 63.9°; minimum 38.9°.

The new Chinaman called at noon. He is a Tung-ling, ranking as a Colonel, and wears a coral button. His name is Chao. He is a cheery, honest looking little man, apparently without any diplomatic pretensions or guile. He chatted away very freely, and gave his views on a number of matters without reserve. Amongst other things he confirmed the common report that the Chinese have lost most of their former prestige amongst the Tibetans, and find great difficulty in having their wishes attended to. He instanced a case which occurred last year at Lhasa where some friction arose between the Tale Lama and the Ambans. What the Colonel said was that, formerly, when there was a Regent, it was the custom for the Ambans to go direct to him concerning any matters which they wished to discuss or arrange; but that now there is no Regent, and they cannot be perpetually worrying a Pontiff like the Tale Lama on secular affairs; whilst if they attempt to give any instructions to the Shapes, they are met by the reply-"We are the servants of the Tale Lama, not of you." The lack of a Regent, he said, caused great inconvenience, as it had "always been a custom to have one." This is, of course, a very perverted view to take of the Tibetan constitution. The "custom" of having a Regent arose from the "custom" of the Regent quietly disposing of the young Tale Lamas when they become old enough to be troublesome. Now that the present Tale Lama has succeeded in attaining his majority, and, instead of being made away with himself, has satisfactorily disposed of his Regent, the political situation at Lhasa has assumed an entirely different complexion. As the power of the Tale Lama increases, so the influence of the Ambans wanes; and all reports tend to confirm the decrease of Chinese prestige throughout Tibet.

Colonel Chao made a long visit of over an hour. On the question of the return call he said that, as he was at present very uncomfortably lodged, he would ask the Commissioners to defer their visit for a day or two.

3rd September.—A cloudy morning. Maximum temperature 70°; minimum 38.9°.

Our flock of sheep with the Lachung shepherd, which has been out grazing all day, has not returned to camp as usual. Two men were sent out to search for it at 10 o'clock P.M.

Political Diary of the Tibet Frontier Commission.
(Extract.)

3rd September, 1903.—Yesterday afternoon Colonel Chao called and said he had been deputed by the Amban to carry on business in the absence of Mr. Ho. He is the Commandant at Phari, from which place he has just arrived. He is about 50 years of age and of the simple, honest, straightforward soldier type. He was very diffident, and full of conversation, informing us that Mr. Ho had been recalled to Lhasa to explain matters to the Chinese Resident. It was not clear whether he had been recalled in disgrace, but the Colonel gave the impression that Mr. Ho had not given satisfaction. I also gathered that he was not to return. But a "clever young civil officer" was to come from Lhasa to help the Colonel.

The new Amban, the Colonel said, was not expected to arrive till November, and the new Assistant Amban would arrive with him.

The Dalai Lama, according to the Colonel, was giving a good deal of trouble to the Chinese Residents. Last year he refused to do what the Resident asked him to do. Formerly Dalai Lamas were always infants, and the Regents always obeyed the Chinese Residents. Now there is an adult Dalai Lama, he does what he likes, and refuses to obey the Resident. Both Residents accordingly last year petitioned the Throne to be relieved of their charges.

The Dalai Lama also wrote a memorial to the Throne, asking to be considered higher than the Tashi Lama of Shigatse, but the Resident refused to forward the petition. The Dalai Lama sits on a seat three feet higher than the Resident. Though his authority is supreme in spiritual matters, the Council assume the chief voice in temporal matters.

The people of Chumbi, the Colonel said, were most anxious for a proper settlement to come out of the present negotiations, as they were hoping trade would thereby increase and their profits with it.

The reply of the Viceroy to the Amban's letter arrived to-day.

4th September.—The Deputy from Shigatse, Bodala by name, came to see Captain O'Connor to-day to say that objections were being raised to our constructing the telegraph line to Khamba Jong. I told Captain O'Connor to say that the telegraph line was being constructed by order of the Viceroy, in order that His Excellency might be able to communicate rapidly with me. It was only a temporary arrangement, and would be removed directly we left here. He might, if he thought necessary, represent this to the Tashi Lama.

5th September. The Shigatse Abbot came to see Captain O'Connor to-day to make a further representation regarding the construction of the telegraph line. These Shigatse people say that personally they do not mind, and they dislike making these constant representations to us; but they are held responsible by the Lhasa authorities, so are bound to make formal protests. They say they are like little birds watching a fight between two wild yaks–the Lhasa Government and ourselves being the yaks.

The Lhasa delegates remain in the fort, and, under orders from Lhasa, decline all intercourse, official or social, with the Commission.

F. E. YOUNGHUSBAND,
British Commissioner.
Khamba Jong,
The 6th September, 1903.

From the Foreign Secretary, Simla, to the Resident in Nepal, Segowlie, Khatmandu, dated the 14th September, 1903.
(Telegraphic.)

Please convey hearty thanks of Government of India to Minister for offer of 500 yaks, which they accept gratefully, and also for cordial cooperation shown by him in addressing admonition and sound advice to Lhasa Government. The Minister's friendly action in this matter is much appreciated. Please inform Younghusband when and how the yaks will move. He wants them in one month at Khamba Jong.

Letter from Colonel F. E. Younghusband, C.I.E., British Commissioner, Tibet Frontier Commission, to the Secretary to the Government of India, in the Foreign Department, dated Khamba Jong, the 9th September, 1903.
(Extract.)

In your telegram, dated 2nd September, you direct me to submit proposals for dealing with the situation if Tibetans continue impracticable. All the information we receive tends to show that the Tibetans do intend to maintain their obstructive attitude. They at present absolutely refuse to negotiate here, and our informant, whom Captain O'Connor had despatched to Lhasa, reports that the head Councillor had declined to serve on the Commission on the ground that war was certain. I think, therefore, it may be taken as assumed that the Tibetans will refuse to negotiate in any way which we could consider satisfactory. That being so, the question arises what action we should take to induce them to change their present attitude. I think the reply of His Excellency the Viceroy to the Amban will have some effect upon the Chinese at least. Both Chinese and Tibetans have no doubt up till now been under the impression that the Commission is merely one more of the futile little missions which have come and gone upon the Sikkim frontier during the last few years. They have thought so far that, if they can be obstruc-

tive enough during the summer and autumn, we will
without doubt return before the winter. The Viceroy's
letter will put them right on that point: and I have also,
in conversation with Mr. Ho and the Shigatse people,
tried to bring both the Chinese and the Tashi Lama
round to putting pressure on the obstinate Lhasa
monks. There is little hope, however, that mere verbal
persuasion will be sufficient. Direct action will be
required. The despatch of a second Pioneer Regiment
to put the road to the Jalap-la in order has, I understand, been ordered. I would recommend that about
the same time my escort should be strengthened by
100 men from the support. But what would have a
greater effect than anything else upon the Tibetans
would be the demonstrating to them that the Nepalese
are on our side, and not on theirs. The Nepalese
Minister has offered 8,000 yaks. I would have 500 of
these march across to us by the Tinki Jong route, and
would recommend that a suitable representative of the
Nepalese Darbar should accompany them for the purpose of formally handing them over to us. This would
be a sign which the Tibetans could not mistake that the
Nepalese were on our side, and the Nepalese Envoy
might be authorised to state this in unmistakable
terms, if necessary, to the Chinese and Tibetan representatives here. The strengthening of my escort and the
appearance of the Nepalese yaks might be made to
coincide with the concentration of the 23rd Pioneers
in the neighbourhood of the Jelap-la Pass in about a
month's time. This is, I think, all that can be done to
bring the Tibetans to a more suitable state of mind. If

these measures fail an advance into the Chumbi valley is the most obvious course to take, for the Jelap-la can be crossed at any time during the winter, and along the Chumbi valley lies the best trade route and military road to Lhasa. When the Chumbi valley has been occupied, the Commission might, transported by the Nepalese yaks, march across to Gyantse. The 32nd Pioneers and all transport would then be transferred to the Chumbi valley line, and that line be for the future made our chief line of communication.

Letter from Colonel F. E. Younghusband, C.I.E., British Commissioner, Tibet Frontier Commission, to the Secretary to the Government of India, in the Foreign Department, dated Khamba Jong, the 4th September, 1903.

With reference to Mr. Russell's letter, dated the 26th August, 1903, I have the honour to report that the letter from His Excellency the Viceroy to His Excellency Yu, which it enclosed, has, together with Chinese and Tibetan translations thereof, been this day forwarded to Captain Parr for transmission to Lhasa.

Political Diary of the Tibet Frontier Commission
(Extract.)

6th September, 1903.—Nil.

7th September.—We all went to pay a return visit to Colonel Chao, who received us in a small tent, and regaled us on milk-punch, which we ourselves, on a hint from him, had sent over for the purpose. He referred again to the construction of the telegraph, but said he had told the Tibetans there was no use in raising objections till the line had actually crossed the frontier. Mr. Wilton tried to come to some arrangement with Colonel Chao concerning the supply of barley and peas to us on payment, urging that, as we were guests in this country, it was only fit that we should be supplied with what we required, at least on payment. Colonel Chao did not, however, give any definite reply.

The villagers are all plucking the barley, though it is not yet thoroughly ripe. It is believed that they are doing this by order-possibly in anticipation of our seizing it, if they allowed it to remain to ripen.

A monk whom Captain O'Connor had sent to Lhasa returned here today with the information that the Lhasa authorities have quite made up their minds to fight, though they will make no move till the late autumn when the crops have been gathered in. The monks are most ready to fight, but the lay authorities say they are not required for the present. Two thousand rifles have been given out; and the people generally been warned to be ready for war.

Further information which the monk brought was to the effect that the Dalai Lama was coming to Shigatse to confer with the Tashi Lama. An unusual number of Mongols are said to be in Lhasa at the present time.

A report was received from Captain Cullen at Tangu that some Tibetans had attempted to stop the telegraph from being constructed beyond Giaogong. He had, however, taken 50 men from Tangu, and informed the Tibetans that we could not allow the construction of the telegraph to be interfered with.

8th September.—Last night Mr. White and Captain O'Connor went off to explore the central range between here and Shigatse.

The ex-monk from Lhasa further stated that the chief Councillor had refused to take part in the Commission on the ground that war was certain, so he could do no good. The Chinese are now-a-days regarded with but small respect, owing to the growing influence of the Dalai Lama.

9th September.—A trustworthy informant says that the chief Councillor has been appointed Chief Commissariat Officer, and is now busily employed in collecting and storing rations for troops in anticipation of hostilities; the informant considers the appointment of these men and the feverish activity displayed in collecting grain indicates that hostilities are inevitable; and from what he has been able to gather, the Tibetans now consider themselves prepared at all points.

F. E. YOUNGHUSBAND, Colonel,
British Commissioner.
Khamba Jong,
The 9th September, 1903.

Diary kept by Captain W. F. O'Connor during the Tibet Frontier Mission
(Extract.)

4th September, 1903.—Bright morning. Horizon clear, but clouds overhead Maximum temperature 65.2°; minimum 41.5°.

The Te-ling Kusho came into camp with word that some of the Tashi-Chempo officials would like to speak to me on one or two minor points. Accordingly, at noon, Ba-du-la and the old Jongpen arrived. After some desultory conversation they raised the question of the telegraph wire which has now progressed beyond Giaogong. Following the usual Tibetan line of argument, they said that it was not the custom to have telegraph wires in Tibet, and they feared they would get into trouble if the line was carried further. They further urged that the additional suspicions which would be aroused by the erection of a telegraph would tend to more delay in the commencement of negotiations. I reported what they said to Colonel Younghusband, who instructed me to inform them that the wire would only be temporary, and would be removed when we left Khamba Jong; that its erection would greatly facilitate the despatch of business when once negotiations began; and that telegraph wires were common in China. He informed them moreover, that the wire was being erected by orders of the Viceroy, and could only be stopped with his sanction. I gave them this message which they said they perfectly understood, but that nevertheless the wire would undoubtedly annoy the Lhasa Government, and raise its suspicions. I said that, in that case, the Amban could very easily explain matters to the Tsong-du and Council, and could allay their suspicions. They laughed at this, and said that, in a matter of this kind, the Amban's representations would have no effect whatever; and that, although the Amban was perfectly aware of the harmless nature of a telegraph wire, he would hesitate to urge any views upon the Lhasa people which were distasteful to their national sentiments. He added that, where Chinese policy was in accordance with their own views, the Tibetans were ready enough to accept the Amban's advice; but that, if this advice ran counter in any respect to their national prejudices, the Chinese Emperor himself would be powerless to influence them. The Tashi-Chempo men throughout behaved and spoke in a most reasonable manner, and before beginning the discussion apologised profusely for the trouble they were giving in raising these "trifling questions." They quite appreciated our common-sense arguments in favour of the wire, but were bound to protest against it for the sake of their own skins. They left promising to report all we had said to the Abbot; and Ba-du-la's last words as he left the tent were:-"The Tsong-du are mad."

About 12.30 p.m. a heavy storm of hail and rain began, which lasted till evening.

Shortly after the Tashi-Chempo men had left our camp, the Khamba Jongpen with a small following, rode off towards Giaogong-no doubt in order to sat-isfy himself regarding the telegraph wire.

Our flock of sheep was brought back to camp late this evening. They had wandered away towards Ta-tsang Gompa. Some 70 were missing, of which a certain number were killed by wolves.

5th September.—There was steady rain during the night, and a light snowfall began about 6 a.m., which lasted till after 8 a.m. Maximum temperature 62.8°; minimum 34°. Total rainfall registered during 24 hours was 1.00 inch.

At noon the Abbot and Ba-du-la came into camp, and I had an interview with them on the matter of the telegraph wire. They had nothing new to urge, and I gave them Colonel Younghusband's reply that, as the wire was being constructed under the Viceroy's orders, the question of stopping it could not be considered unless raised by the Amban or the Tibetan Government. With this they were obliged to be satisfied; but they said that their position between the British and Tibetan Governments was a very difficult one, and they compared themselves to a little boy who tries to interfere in a quarrel between two wild yaks with the probable result of getting his leg broken. They went away, saying that they would represent the case to the Lhasa officers-from whom, however, they do not seem to anticipate very much.

6th September.—This is a clearer morning than we have had for some time. The snows of the Sikkim frontier are visible, but with wreaths of cloud rising here and there. A good deal of fresh snow has fallen on the lower slopes of the southern Himalayas and on the central chain. The Sebubu-La, and the road thence towards Giaogong is all under snow.

Maximum temperature 54.2°; minimum 32.2°. Rain
.03 inches.

The Jongpen rode back towards the Jong from
the direction of Giaogong about 8 a.m. Colonel
Younghusband and Mr. Bailey rode out towards the
hot springs to collect natural history specimens, and
Mr. White took some photographs of the Jong, &c. In
the afternoon the wind changed, and blew from the
north for the first time since we have been here,
blowing back heavy masses of clouds towards the
Sikkim frontier, and having the mountains of the central chain quite clear. This looks as if the monsoon
currents had been defeated at last, and that we are in
for the spell of clear weather to which we are entitled
at this time of the year.

No further protest has been made either by the
Tashi-Chempo or Lhasa officials regarding the telegraph wire. The Jongpen, it appears, tried his usual
obstructive tactics with the working party, but was
told to clear out, and not make himself a nuisance. A
party from Tangu has removed another small collection of Tibetans from Giaogong.

7th September.—A glorious clear morning. Not a
cloud in the sky, and all the snows showing up plainly.
It froze last night for the first time since 7th July-the
day we arrived here. Maximum temperature 62.8° ;
minimum 28.5°.

At 10 a.m. the Commissioner, accompanied by
Mr. Wilton and myself, called on Colonel Chao at his
tent near Captain Parr's camp. Captain Parr was also

present. The conversation was confined to general topics. The people here have begun to pluck their barley, although it is not yet ripe. Instead of reaping it in the usual manner, they pluck it up by the roots, and have left it out on the fields to dry. The only explanation I can think of for this proceedings is that they have been ordered to pull up their barley before it ripens by way of rendering it impossible for us to get grain on the spot later on. It is a most unfortunate thing that we should have been obliged to be dependent for our supply of grain for so long on these people.

During the day I arranged for a short trip to the central range, as I was anxious to obtain a view northwards from the summit of one of the peaks. Mr. White decided to accompany me, and accordingly we started at 7.30 p.m. just as the moon rose, and, accompanied by four followers and one led-mule, rode in a N.N.W. direction along the track leading to Utsi Gompa. It was a lovely night-bright moonlight-almost as light as day, and we had no difficulty in finding our way. As we had kept our proceedings quite secret, no attempt was made to stop us, and we encountered only a few coolies near the Jong. Giving Utsi Monastery and village a wide berth we continued in the same general direction past the village of Kyerong (12 miles), and then turning almost due north steered by the stars and the distant peaks of the central chain. Our way lay over a series of level plains and low scrub-covered spurs and across some deep wide dry nulla beds-which latter puzzled us a good deal at the time. Soon after midnight we reached the bed of a stream which drains the southern slopes of this portion of the chain and flows westwards into the Tsomo-tel-tung lake. We followed up this stream for some two or three miles until we were well into the foothills of the range and near the mouth of the side-nulla which we decided to follow up next day, and at 1.20 a.m. we pitched our small tente-d'abri in a sheltered corner. Elevation 15,600 feet. Distance from Khamba Jong estimated 21 miles.

8th September.—There was a very heavy dew where we camped, and everything left outside the tent was soaked. It froze pretty hard during the night, and the ground was all white with hoar-frost in the morning. I put out my small travelling thermometer before going to sleep, but Mr. White's Lepcha servant found it lying about and carefully shut it up in its box and put it away-so I failed to get the temperature. (Maximum temperature at Khamba Jong 63°; minimum 35°.) It was a lovely clear morning, not a cloud in the sky, and Mr. White and I, starting off at 7 a.m., rode still northwards up the bed of the stream, and crossing a small side-nulla (where there was a large "dok" or shepherd's encampment), we struck into the valley which we decided to follow to its source in the mountains. We left our servants to follow behind and to camp in a nice spot near the foot of the hills. The valley we were now in ran in a general N.N.W. direction curving due N. near the top. It extended altogether some 6 or 7 miles with a flat grassy bottom throughout widening at the mouth to a broad pasture land, half a mile or more in width, where herds of sheep and yaks were grazing. We rode quietly up the valley and reached the pass at the top at 10.20 a.m. Elevation 18,900 feet, distance from our last camp about 10 miles. To our disappointment there was no view obtainable from the pass–two spurs ran out east and west of us, and their crests hid all the country to the north. Accordingly I made my way to a saddle on the east, and thence climbed a peak to the south, and from the summit (just 20,000 feet by aneroid barometer) obtained a good view of the part of Tibet lying north and north and north-east.

From north to north-east the horizon was bounded by a low range of mountains whose average height I estimate at 18,000 to 19,000 feet but, at their north-east extension a huge snowy peak showed up rising apparently from behind the low range and exhibiting several thousand feet of snow. It is certainly a very lofty peak. Another peak also situated at a great distance beyond the range was visible to the N.N.E. The valleys draining north run down steeply in narrow gorges with grassy hillsides, and flow into the wide grassy valley of the Rhe Chu just visible far below. The country is mountainous, but the streams descend steeply to a comparatively low elevation, and their beds must unquestionably be more fertile than the barren region which lies to the south of the central chain, and in which we are now camped. I enjoyed a view of unparalleled magnificence for half an hour, and descended again to the pass after taking a round of photographs. We rode down the valley and reached our little camp at 4.30 p.m. Some 10 or 11 armed men having arrived at the village near our camp, we took precautions against a night attack or the theft of our ponies.

9th September.–A lovely bright cloudless morning. (Maximum temperature at Khamba Jong 68.2°; minimum 30.5°.) Some villagers approached our camp and begged us to go away. Starting at 6.30 a.m. we rode southwards towards Khamba Jong, taking a line somewhat to the east of our first road. This led across a lofty plateau into the plain of the Chi Chu, and we reached Khamba Jong at 4.30 p.m. without incident. We crossed several sheltered valleys, where grazing and firewood are very abundant. The only game we saw during our expedition was goa and hares and two prowling wolves. The views obtained have given us a very good conception of the topography of all this part of Tibet.

10th September.—Lovely bright morning. Maximum temperature 70.9°: minimum 33°.

Quiet day in camp. Our mess-tent having at length arrived, was pitched to-day.

Political Diary of Tibet Frontier Commission
(Extract.)

10th September, 1903.—Mr. White and Captain O'Connor returned last night from their expedition in the Shigatse direction. They report that the country descends steeply on the other side of the central range towards Shigatse. All the valleys and hillsides are well covered with grass, and there are numerous and large flocks of sheep grazing.

The weather has been slightly warmer to-day. The minimum last night was 33 degrees; and the maximum in the sun has been 81 degrees. Heavy storms are sweeping along the Himalayas.

12th September.—A Chinaman informed Mr. Wilton that the Tibetans were beginning to get alarmed, and were by no means so confident as they were. He also said that the new Assistant Amban had returned to China from the borders of Tibet. It had long been suspected that he meant to get out of joining his appointment if he possibly could. No Chinese official likes coming to Tibet.

Ba–du–la, the Shigatse Deputy, came to see Captain O'Connor to-day. The Lhasa delegates know that the Viceroy has refused to recognise them, and Ba–du–la says that, if we would go to Yatung proper, delegates would at once come to us. He also says that the Abbot has consulted the horoscope, and finds that Yatung is a most favourable place for negotiations. He and other Tibetans spoke in the most disparaging terms of the Chinese, and said the way they demanded ponies, supplies, firewood, &c., without paying for it was a great hardship.

13th September.—The telegraph line constructed by Mr. McMahon reached camp this evening; and the

highest telegraph station in the world has been established. The height of Khamba Jong, according to
computations by the Survey of India of observations
by Mr. White, is 15,722 feet above the sea–almost
exactly the height of Mont Blanc.

> F. E. YOUNGHUSBAND,
> British Commissioner.
> Khamba Jong,
> The 14th September, 1903.

*From His Britannic Majesty's Minister, Peking, to His
Excellency the Viceroy, Simla, dated the 23rd September,
1903.*
(Telegraphic.)

The British Consul-General at Cheng-tu reports new
Resident for Tibet at that place. He will start for his
post about the 8th of October.

*From His Britannic Majesty's Minister, Peking, to His Excell-
ency the Viceroy, Simla, dated the 28th September, 1903.*
(Telegraphic.)

The Consul-General at Chengtu reports that the new
Resident was instructed to consult new Viceroy of
Szechuen regarding Tibet affairs; delay was partly
owing to this. The new Assistant Resident, who was
also at Chengtu, proposed to take a large number of
troops, but the Viceroy, then Resident, protested.
Latter proceeding to his post 11th October, with an
escort of some forty soldiers. The Assistant Resident's

departure is not yet fixed.

Diary kept by Captain W. F. O'Connor during the Tibet Frontier Mission.
(Extract.)

11th September 1903.—Bright, clear, cloudless morning. Maximum temperature 71°; minimum 30°.

A large convoy arrived bringing parcels, stores &c. Large quantities of provisions continue to arrive at the Jong. On the 5th instant, 85 yak-loads of salt and tsampa arrived; on the 8th, 70 yak-loads; on the 10th, 35 yak-loads; and smaller quantities on the intermediate days. The salt is exchanged with the villagers for grain. If this activity is typical of what is going on all over Tibet, the Tibetan Commissariat Department will be well supplied when hostilities begin; and we shall know where to forage for supplies.

12th September.—Cloudless morning. Maximum temperature 69.9°; minimum 32.5°.

One of the servants reports that after the moon rose last night, he saw a large number of Tibetans crossing the pass over the hill to the north of the Jong, coming from the Shigatse direction. He says they came in batches of 10 and 20 at a time, and must have numbered several hundreds. He thinks they all went into the Jong.

The telegraph wire is now progressing apace, and the posts are all up as far as this. The wire should be in to-morrow.

Ba-du-la and the old and present Jongpens called at 3 this afternoon, and the Kumar and I had a long conversation with them. They only came to have a talk, I think, but, of course, raised their usual complaints. As an additional argument in favour of the adoption of Yatung as a place of meeting, Ba-du-la said that the Abbot had recently cast a most excellent horoscope by which it had been revealed to him that Yatung was in every respect admirably situated for the discussion of frontier affairs, and, in fact, a better place could scarcely be found. I told him that this fact would certainly be borne in mind and given due weight in future consideration of the subject. He also said that should the Amban and a Shape come here as he believed was proposed, the local people would be put to the greatest trouble and hardship in supplying these officials and their retinue with fuel and provisions. That the Chinese especially were too proud to burn the ordinary sheep or yak-dung fuel, and would have to be supplied with wood, and he said that the Chinese officials were extortionate and mean. That they got all they could from the poor country-people and never paid a penny for anything. There is little love lost between them and the Tibetans.

13th September.—Bright, cloudless morning. Maximum temperature 66.5°; minimum 28°.

Mr. White and I, starting at 10.35, rode to Giru and thence, leaving the main road to Sikkim, we turned a little to the eastward and rode on to the hills of the Sikkim frontier, and descended to the half-way hut on the Sikkim side. A piercing cold wind was blowing up the Lachen valley from the south, and we contrasted the climate most unfavourably with that of Khamba Jong. When our yaks reached us, we went on and camped near Gyamtso Nong-17,200 feet.

14th September.—The wind blew without intermission all night. In fact, the Lachen valley is a regular funnel, confined by the two great peaks of Kangchenjhao and Chomiomo on the east and west, up which pours a continuous stream of fog and mist accompanied by a howling wind. We could see this valley smoking like a great chimney from other parts of Tibet and Sikkim, when the sky elsewhere was perfectly cloudless. Minimum temperature at our camp, 24°.

[Maximum temperature at Khamba Jong 64°; minimum 28.5°.]

Starting at 9 A.M. we rode along eastwards, just inside the Sikkim frontier, and camped after a 13 mile march at Oloteng Dok, just north of the Donkhya Pass. Elevation 18,300 feet.

15th September.—Bright, clear morning. Minimum temperature during the night 19.5°. Temperature at 6.30 A.M. 25°.

[Maximum temperature at Khamba Jong 67°; minimum 30.5°.]

Leaving camp at 7.30 A.M., we travelled in a south-easterly direction to the summit of the

Kangchung La, where we made hypsometrical observations. From the summit of the pass we had a fair
view of Tibet to north and north-east. The general
character of the country is far more mountainous
than I had supposed, the hills rising 2,000 and 3,000
feet above the valley bottoms. Leaving the yaks to
continue down the valley to the north-east, Mr.
White and I rode up the hillside to the east to a
height of some 20,000 feet, whence we could see
Chumolbari and the Bham Tso on the main
Chumbi-Gyangtse road. We descended thence along
the ridge to a "dok" or shepherds' encampment at the
junction of four streams some 8 or 9 miles from the
summit of the pass.

On arrival here we found that our yak-drivers
had mistaken their orders and gone astray, and we sent
off our only attendant (my Tibetan servant) to hunt
for them. It was now getting dark, so we resigned
ourselves to a night in the open and soon lit a good
fire of yak-dung. Just at dark a small party of Tibetans
sneaked up to our camp and took us by surprise; but
they were very civil, and withdrew when we told
them to come again in the morning. By nine o'clock
our yaks and servants turned up. Elevation of our
camp 17,000 feet.

16th September.—Clear, cloudless morning.
Minimum temperature during the night 18.2°.

[Maximum temperature at Khamba Jong 67.5°;
minimum 30°.]

We found quite a crowd of Tibetans gathered

round us in the morning, some 50 or 60 altogether, and they kept dropping in by twos and threes until we started. They were most of them "soldiers," without arms of any kind, and as simple and good-natured a collection of young yokels as we could wish to meet. They made no attempt to interfere with us in any way, only asking us to go back or they would get into trouble. We announced our intention of going straight across country to Khamba Jong, to which they cheerfully acquiesced-only too thankful to be rid of us at any price. They were under the orders of a "Shengo" or "Dingpon." After forming them up in line and photographing them, we rode off in an easterly direction towards Ta-tsang Gompa. Our escort accompanied us for a mile or two, and we parted on the best of terms. These so-called soldiers were all Gyangtse men brought here to watch the passes. They are simple and a collection of ignorant untrained rustics without the slightest pretensions towards military acquirements and apparently without arms. Their one idea of military science is to build ridiculous little breast-walls on the crests of passes and across the roads. After a short march of some seven miles, we camped on the banks of a stream some five miles south of Ta-tsang Gompa.

17th September.—Clear morning. Minimum temperature 24°.

[Maximum temperature at Khamba Jong 73°; minimum 33.5°.]

Sending our baggage to Ta-tsang Gompa, we rode

in a north-easterly direction for some seven miles to the summit of a pass in the central chain whence we obtained a good view of the Kala Tso and the country in the neighbourhood. There was the usual Tibetan guard at the top of the pass and the usual breastworks defending the pass and the hills on either side. The Kala Tso lies in a wide open basin surrounded by hills on all sides. Round the shores of the lake are green marshy-looking expanses, with a "dok" here and there, but no houses or villages visible. Neither in the plain of the lake, nor on the surrounding hillsides, could we see any trace of "Yomo" or other fuel. The Gyangtse road lies along the eastern shores of the lake across a level plain, and then enters what appeared to us a narrow gorge with high steep hills on either side. We chatted freely with the Tibetan soldiers, and they gave us the benefit of such topographical knowledge as they possessed. The pass we were in is called the Lombo La, elevation 16,950 feet. It is reached by an easy gradient on either side, and the stream flowing to the east drains into the Kala Tso through an open grassy valley. This is certainly the easiest way to reach the Kala Tso either from Giru or from Khamba Jong. Making a slight detour, we rode to our camp at Ta-tsang Gompa, which we reached at 2 P.M., shooting a Kyang en route.

In the evening we visited Ta-tsang Gompa, which is an "Ani Gompa," or nunnery containing 36 nuns. These good ladies received us without the smallest embarrassment, and allowed us to take their photographs and to converse with them freely. They ranged through all ages from 10 to 80, and were most of them incredibly dirty; but some of the younger women were quite pretty, and all were most cheerful and friendly. After visiting their place of worship, we distributed some rupees, and left with a promise to send them some tea, &c., as a present from Khamba.

The Gompa is built on a rock by the side of a nice stream of water which flows here in a grassy valley.

18th September.—It clouded up during the night, and there were heavy banks of clouds all round and overhead in the morning. Minimum temperature 33°.

[Maximum temperature at Khamba Jong 71°; minimum 39°.]

We paid a second visit to the nunnery before starting and took some more photographs. Starting at 8.45 a.m., we rode quietly into Khamba Jong, a distance of about 20 miles. Keeping to the south of the range of hills bounding the Khamba Jong nulla, we crossed a very elevated plateau sloping gradually upwards for some seven or eight miles, and covered with herds of kyang and goa. We reached our camp at 2 p.m., just in time to escape a heavy fall of hail which whitened all the hills behind us. The yaks took nine hours to cover the distance.

As a result of our trip, we have made ourselves thoroughly acquainted with the country to the east of this place as far as the crest of the hills separating the basin of the Arun from the streams flowing into the Kala Tso, and can now move in the direction of

Gyangtse over routes which we know. As regards the fuel question, there is no fuel (except the usual small quantities of yak-dung) between Khamba Jong and Kala Tso. A force moving in that direction would have to carry at least four days' fuel. Native information says that, on leaving Kala Tso, scrub bushes of sorts are found in plenty all the way to Gyangtse.

Major Bretherton and Captain Mackie, I.M.S., rode into camp from Tangu during the evening.

From the Resident in Nepal, Segowlie, to Colonel F. E. Younghusband, C.I.E. Khamba Jong, dated the 27th September, 1903.
(Telegraphic.)

Yaks will be sent as desired viâ Wallung to Tipta La Pass. Colonel Harak Jang, Ilam, instructed to inform you direct of probable date of arrival.

From His Britannic Majesty's Minister, Peking, to His Excellency the Viceroy, Simla, dated the 1st October, 1903.
(Telegraphic.)

I have received the following telegram from the Consul at Chengtu:-"The Resident for Tibet says that, to reach the Indian frontier, it will take at least three months."

From the Foreign Secretary, Simla, to Colonel F. E. Young-husband, C.I.E., Khamba Jong, dated the 2nd October, 1903.
(Telegraphic.)

Colonel J. R. L. Macdonald, C.B., Commanding Royal Engineers, Quetta District, has been appointed Commanding Royal Engineer on road from Siliguri onwards under the orders of Director-General, Military Works. Colonel Macdonald will assume command, as senior officer on spot, of all troops employed on road from Siliguri onwards, with exception of actual escort of Mission and its support.

Political Diary of the Tibet Frontier Commission.
(Extract.)

21st September, 1903.—Mr. Hayden, of the Geological Survey, arrived to-day. He has examined the fossils which Mr. White had collected, and says they belong to the Jurassic period and very similar to those found in the Spiti shales. As they are marine, they prove, of course, that all this country was some million of years ago under the sea. Mr. Hayden says that the geological formation about here is not such as would be favourable for the discovery of gold. He has entered Tibet before at the head of the Sutlej Valley, and says the country there is very similar to this.

22nd September.—Lieutenant Mackie returned to Tangu (Major Bretherton returned there on the 20th).

Ba-du-la, the Shigatse Deputy, came to see Captain O'Connor, who, by direction, informed him of the contents of the letter from the Nepalese Minister to the Lhasa Council. He made no remark on it, but Captain O'Connor says he spoke of the Napalese as being very friendly with the Tibetans.

The villagers are ploughing the land from which they have recently cut the crops.

24th September.—Major Prain, I.M.S., Director of the Botanical Gardens, Calcutta, and Captain Walton, I.M.S., arrived to-day.

Captain Parr received a letter from the Amban, saying that he intended to come here, but that he had not received an answer yet from the Dalai Lama in regard to the appointment of Tibetan representatives.

26th September.-I accompanied Major Prain and Mr. Hayden on an expedition to the hot springs. On the way we met four Tibetans with carpets thrown over their backs. On our offering to buy the carpets, if they would bring them to camp, they said they were not allowed to go near the camp, but had to take everything they had for sale to the Jongpen first, and, needless to say, he would take a good commission from them before he would allow them to sell at all. We accordingly paid them money on the spot and carried off the carpets on our ponies. The Tibetans were delighted, and we went away feeling that this was only one more object-lesson proving that the Tibetans are perfectly ready to be friendly with us and to do business with us, if only the Lamas and officials did not keep us apart.

Captain Parr informed me that Mr. Ho had been greatly delayed on his way to Lhasa, owing to the Tibetans refusing to supply him with carriage, on the grounds that he had failed in the present negotiations, and therefore deserved no assistance from them. This shows both the small respect the Tibetans now have for the Chinese, and also that the negotiations up till now are not considered a success by the opposite party.

Diary kept by Captain W. F. O'Connor during the Tibet Frontier Mission.
(Extract.)

19th September, 1903.—Clear morning. Maximum temperature 74.8°; minimum 30.5°.

No news of any kind. I forgot to mention that the Kumar has returned to Sikkim. He left the camp on the 14th, but proposes to return later on. The Teling Kusho asked leave to send a telegram to the Kumar to-day, which he did, and presently received a reply to his great satisfaction.

A trustworthy informant says that the Depon being still unwell has received permission to leave Khamba Jong and will shortly depart.

20th September.—Clear morning. Maximum temperature 76.5°; minimum 31°. There was a heavy hailstorm at 2 p.m.

Major Bretherton left after breakfast for Tangu. Mr. Wilton and Captain Parr started off on a trip in the direction of Ta-tsang Gompa. A convoy arrived in the evening bringing parcels, which included some fresh meteorological instruments.

21st September.—Heavy clouds overhead and all

around except to the south over the Sikkim frontier. Maximum temperature 70.5°; minimum 37.5°. Rain .13 inches.

Mr. Hayden, of the Geological Survey Department, arrived here to-day from Tangu. Lieutenant Mackie, I.M.S., returned to Tangu.

22nd September.—Cloudy morning. Maximum temperature 75°; minimum 36°. Rain .01 inches.

At 12 o'clock Ba-du-la, the old Jongpen, and the Teling Kusho called. I received them in my tent and had a long conversation with them. They are very anxious to know the result of the Viceroy's despatch to the Amban, and having heard that Captain Parr has received a letter from the Amban, they came to ask whether this was a reply to the despatch. Having explained to them that this was only a private letter, I proceeded, in the course of conversation, to ask them about Tibet's relations with Nepal. They assured me that the Nepalese and Tibetans were on the friendliest terms, and that they were acquainted with the terms of the treaty by which Nepal was bound to help Tibet in case of foreign invasion. On this I translated to them (as instructed by Colonel Younghusband) the letter from the Nepalese Prime Minister to the Tale Lama, of which a copy had been forwarded to Colonel Younghusband by the Foreign Department. The Tashi Lumpo officials listened with the greatest interest, and appeared to appreciate the force of the Prime Minister's arguments and to understand the general tenour of the letter. When I translated the portion, in which the Prime Minister says that he proposes to assist Tibet merely by advice, the Tibetan officers laughed heartily, and said that they were in very much the same position themselves: that the Tashi Lumpo Government was unable to do much more than offer advice to the Lhasa authorities. They made no other remarks upon the contents of the letter, but followed each item of the Prime Minister's "advice" intently, checking off the various paragraphs, and explaining doubtful points to one another. They appeared especially impressed by the concluding paragraph regarding the forbearance of the English in religious matters and the discovery of Buddha's birthplace in Nepal owing to the researches of Englishmen. I asked them what they thought would be done as to sending other representatives from Lhasa. They said that it would be impossible to send any more high officials to Khamba Jong; that the people round about here had already been squeezed to the limits of endurance (neither Chinese nor Tibetan officials pay for any of the supplies provided for themselves, followers, or animals); and that, if any more dignitaries should arrive here, the country people would all run away. They think it probable, however, that fresh delegates may be deputed to meet us at Yatung. The Depon, they said, is very ill indeed, and the services of 50 monks have been secured to pray continually for his recovery. After our conversation we all went to inspect the Telegraph Office, which pleased them greatly, and after admiring Mr. Mitter's type-writer, they took their departure. These Shigatse men thoroughly enjoy strolling round our camp, examining such curious objects as glass windows, stoves, sepoys, &c.-it is as great a treat to them as a country fair is to our English rustic. I presented them each with the inevitable photograph which they seem to appreciate more than anything else, and the Hospital Assistant prescribed for Ba-du-la, who has a boil on his leg.

23rd September.—Cloudy morning. Some rain fell during the night-.03 inches registered. Maximum teperature 66°; minimum 39°.

The Jongpen called during the morning regarding the question of the grazing here. He says that the local people are now bringing in their sheep and goats to graze round about the Jong; and, under the circumstances, he thinks some fresh arrangement is desirable concerning the rent which we are paying for the grazing. He assumed a very humble tone (quite different from his original truculent attitude); said that he had heard that we had complained at paying so high a price for the grazing rights, and that for the future he did not want to take anything from us at all. As instructed by Colonel Younghusband, I told him that we quite understood that the peasants required the use of their grazing lands, and that, under the circumstances, we should raise no objection to their flocks coming here, but would, with his consent, reduce the rate we were paying for the grazing to one half; and that, as regards the amount paid, we were giving it not only for the grazing rights, but also in consideration of the Jongpen's own services in procuring grain, sheep, &c., for us. The Jongpen seemed pleased with this answer, and went off saying that he would consult with his tenants, and would give us an answer on the following day. He says that the Depon has asked for leave to return to Lhasa, but has not yet received permission to do so.

Mr. Wilton and Captain Parr returned from their expedition in the direction of Ta-tsang, having shot one kyang and one ovis ammon.

The weather keeps very cloudy and dark, and there appears to be heavy rain to the south. We are treated to a hailstorm nearly every afternoon.

We sent off a man to Ta-tsang with a yak carrying "tsampa," tea, butter, and salt as a present to the nuns.

24th September.—Cloudy morning. Maximum temperature 68°; minimum 31°. Rain .08 inches.

Mr. White left camp at 8.30 a.m. for Tangu. He expects to be absent for a month or so in Sikkim and Darjeeling. At about noon the Teling Kusho called on me at my request, and we had an hour's conversation. I learnt nothing new from him politically, but he is always an interesting man to talk to, with a plentiful store of anecdotes. I am anxious, too, to accustom myself to the Tsang dialect which differs materially from that of Lhasa. Major Prain, Director of Botanical Surveys in India, and Captain Walton, I.M.S. (our new medical officer), arrived to-day. Our man returned from Ta-tsang, bringing most grateful messages from the nuns for our present. He says they were delighted, and have promised to perform a variety of different religious services on our behalf. Mr. Hayden made an excursion up the Khamba Jong nulla. He has already discovered a great number of fossils and other interesting geological specimens.

25th September.—Dark, cloudy morning. Maximum temperature 64°; minimum 35°.

Colonel Younghusband and Major Prain made a short botanizing excursion, and Mr. Hayden also was out all day on the hills. There was a shower at 3.30 p.m. and drizzling rain again in the evening. The weather keeps very threatening with heavy clouds overhead and daily storms of rain and hail.

26th September.—Still cloudy. Maximum temperature 63.5°; minimum 36.5°. Rain .05 inches.

Colonel Younghusband, Major Prain, and Mr. Hayden made an excursion to the Kozo hot springs and were out all day till evening. Captain Walton and Mr. Wilton also went out along the foot of the hills bounding the south side of the Khamba Jong nulla, and shot a couple of burrhel.

About 12 o'clock the Teling Kusho called on me and we had an hour's chat on general topics. A little later the old and present Jongpens joined us, and the question of the payment for the Khamba Jong grazing was settled. The Jongpen said that he had talked the matter over with Ba-du-la and the other Tashi Lumpo officials, and that they had instructed him not to take any further rent from us. I told him that

Colonel Younghusband would be very pleased to continue to make him a monthly allowance not only for the grazing, but in consideration of his other services to us. But the Jongpen said that he could take no further monthly payment. If we would pay him up to date at the original rate, and continue to purchase such supplies as he could give us, he would be very well satisfied. I agreed to do this, but begged him to remember that the arrangement was of his own choice, and not due to any desire on our part to put an end to the bargain; and I told him that later on, if he found that his peasants were being oppressed or were grumbling about their grazing rights, he should come to us and let us know, in order that we might be able to make a fresh arrangement. He appeared very grateful and thanked me profusely. In fact, his demeanour is far more subdued than it was when we first made his acquaintance. There can be no doubt that he and the other local people cannot help contrasting our methods very favourably with those of their own and the Chinese officials.

Mr. Harrison, the Postmaster-General of Bengal, arrived in camp in the evening from Tangu.

From Colonel F. E. Younghusband, C.I.E., Khamba Jong, to the Foreign Secretary, Simla, dated the 7th October, 1903. (Telegraphic.)

I propose to strengthen my escort by hundred men from the supports as soon as transport can be conveniently obtained.

From Colonel F. E. Younghusband, C.I.E., Khamba Jong, to the Foreign Secretary, Simla, dated the 8th October, 1903.
(Telegraphic.)

Viceroy's despatch reached Amban one month ago, and no reply has yet been received, though letters from Lhasa can reach here in four days. Mission has been here three months without being able to even commence negotiations. Chinese show indifference and incompetence, and Tibetans show pure obstruction. Present Amban is acknowledged by even Chinese to be weak and incompetent, and his Assistant Amban was allowed to resign some months ago. New Amban, though appointed last December, will only leave Chengtu to-day, and cannot reach frontier before January. New Assistant Amban has been given sick leave before even joining his post. Mr. Ho, though I had given him the very serious warning mentioned in my diaries of the 1st and 2nd September, made no haste to proceed to Lhasa, but loitered at Phari. Wai-Wu-Pu could send a telegram to Amban, on Sir E. Satow's warning of 25th September, through here, to Lhasa, and I might by now have heard from Amban in regard to it, but no such telegram has passed through here. Even if the Chinese show less indifference, they could do little with the Tibetans. Mr. Ho was refused transport by the Tibetans, and Colonel Chao tells me new Amban could not bring large number of troops to Tibet, as Tibetans would refuse to furnish transport and supplies. As regards the attitude of Tibetans, though people round here and the Shigatse Deputies are perfectly friendly, the Lhasa authorities are as obstructive as ever. The Lhasa delegates, since the first formal visits, have refused all communication, social or official, with me. The two prisoners remain in custody, and Tibetan troops line all the heights between here and Gyangtse or Shigatse. The Tibetans refuse to negotiate here, and are preparing to resist any advance further into Tibet. There is much probability that Siberian Buriat Lamas are present in Lhasa. After the Sikkim war, we showed moderation in hopes of good results ensuing from a considerate need [sic]. In the following year, we continued the same patient policy. During the past three months, I have exercised all the patience of which I am capable. The results of all this moderation are nil, and I can no longer hold out any hope to Government of a peaceful solution of this question.

From Colonel F. E. Younghusband, C.I.E., Khamba Jong, to the Foreign Secretary, Simla, dated the 10th October, 1903.
(Telegraphic.)

Report received and confirmed by Deputy Commissioner, Darjeeling, that Lhasa Government have forbidden Tibetans to sell ponies and mules at Kalimpong Fair this year. I hear they have also forbidden sale of wool, but so far Deputy Commissioner has not heard of this report.

From Colonel F. E.Younghusband, C.I.E., Khamba Jong, to the Foreign Secretary, Simla, dated the 10th October, 1903.
(Telegraphic.)

Representation received from missionaries in Lachung, saying the people are paralysed with fear at the seizure of the two men by the Shigatse people three months ago, who, it is reported, have been tortured and cut in pieces. Missionaries represent that Lachung people are largely dependent on trade with Shigatse, but now dare not cross the border, and the distress of the people is so great that they have been compelled to voice the feelings of the people. I have informed missionaries of the action which has already been taken by Government.

From the Foreign Secretary, Simla, to Colonel F. E. Younghusband, C.I.E., Gangtok, dated the 12th October, 1903.
(Telegraphic.)

Do you know at what place the Lachung men are actually detained as prisoners by the Tibetans?

Political Diary of the Tibet Frontier Commission.
(Extract.)

28th September, 1903.—The Abbot lunched with the Mission. He was very cheery, but assured us that he had made a divination that Yatung was the place where negotiations would be carried through quickest. I said we wanted to find a place where they would be carried through not quickest, but best, and asked him to consult his beads again, and see if Shigatse would not be suitable in that respect. But he laughed and replied that the divination had to be made in front of an altar to the accompaniment of music. Captain O'Connor has succeeded in making the Abbot and his people extremely friendly: so much so that Mr. Wilton has heard from Chinese sources that the Chinese believe we have either bought over the Abbot or promised them some considerable concession.

29th September.—Mr. Hayden left camp to study the geology round the Tso-Lamo lake.

30th September.—I rode over to Tangu with Major Prain. He is very well satisfied with the results of his botanical tour, and has discovered many more plants than he had expected to find.

1st October.—I returned from Tangu.

3rd October.—Mr. Hayden returned to camp.
    F. E. YOUNGHUSBAND,
    British Commissioner.
    Khamba Jong,
    The 5th October, 1903.

Diary kept by Captain W. F. O'Connor during the Tibet Frontier Mission.

(Extract.)

27th September, 1903.—Bright sunny morning; very pleasant after all the cloudy weather we have had lately. Maximum temperature 56.4°; minimum 31.5°.

Colonel Younghusband, Major Prain, and Mr. Hayden made an expedition up to the head of the Khamba Jong nulla, and returned along the foot of the hills bounding the nulla on the south.

Mr. Bailey has gone to Tangu on a few days' leave, and Captain Cooke has come over for a visit from the reserve of the 32nd Pioneers at Tangu.

28th September.—Bright cloudless morning. Maximum temperature 67.4°; minimum 27.9°.

An invitation was sent to the Abbot, Ba-du-la, and the Te-ling Kusho to come to lunch. They arrived in camp about noon, and we entertained them for an hour with the gramophone, and by showing them Major Prain's and Mr. Hayden's collections of plants and fossils, and Mr. Harrison also took their photographs. The Abbot was good enough to recite a prayer into the gramophone, thus giving us a valuable record. He amused us at lunch by giving us an account of how he conducted his little prophecies and obtained glimpses into the future. This he does with the aid chiefly of his rosary, and he told us that he had discovered that negotiations at Khamba Jong would be a long and unsatisfactory business, but would be conducted far more readily at Yatung. All three gentlemen were very pleased with their reception, and left after tiffin, after first making the round of the camp and visiting the telegraph office, &c.

At about 6.30 p.m. we had a heavy squall from the north bringing thunder and hail, which lasted about half an hour.

29th September.—Bright cloudless morning. Maximum temperature 68°; minimum 31° Rain .09 inches.

Major Prain, Mr. Harrison, and I starting at 9 a.m. rode out north-west to the Pari hill, which I had previously visited with Mr. White. We rode up to the top of the hill, whence we obtained a good view of the Tsomo-tel-tung lake, Major Prain collecting some botanical specimens en route-amongst other specimens of the various bushes which grow so freely on this hillside, and which are of especial interest from their value as fuel. Mr. Harrison and I shot some hares, partridges, and a fine lammer-geir on our way down, and we rode home across the Khamba plain reaching camp at 6 p.m. Weather absolutely perfect, except for a sudden hailstorm which caught us on our way home. Major Prain has kindly taken specimens of each of the qualities of brick-tea I have collected here, which he will take with him to Calcutta for analysis.

Mr. Hayden started off this morning towards Ta-tsang Gompa on a geological tour, and intends to return via Tso-lamo.

Captain Parr dined with us.

30th September.—Bright cloudless morning. Maximum temperature 66.4°; minimum 28.9°.

Temperatures during the month of September were as follows:-

Average maximum temperature67.08°

Highest ,, ,,76.5°

Average minimum temperature33.16°

Lowest ,, ,,27.9°

Rainfall during the month1.46

Total rainfall up to date (July, August, and September)4.192

Major Prain left this morning for Tangu. Colonel Younghusband accompanies him as far as Tangu, and returns to-morrow. Mr. Harrison spent the day out on the hills after burrhel and goa.

1st October.—A fine morning, but clouds over the hills of the Sikkim frontier. Maximum temperature 64.9°; minimum 30.5°.

Mr. Harrison, Captain Walton, and myself spent the day shooting some five or six miles from camp, and made a good bag of 54 hares and some partridges and sand-grouse. Colonel Younghusband returned from Tangu in the evening.

2nd October.—Raw damp morning with clouds overhead, and on the surrounding hills. Maximum temperature 65.6°; minimum 29.8°.

Mr. Harrison left this morning for Tangu en route to Calcutta. Mr. Bailey returned from Tangu in the afternoon.

3rd October.—Cloudy morning. Maximum temperature 56.8°; minimum 32.5°.

The Te-ling Kusho called in the course of the morning and, as instructed by Colonel Younghusband, I handed over to him a handsome gold watch which Colonel Younghusband had procured from Calcutta as a present for the Tashi Lama. The Tashi Lama had previously sent two very old gold watches to us, asking us to have them repaired and put in order for him, and Colonel Younghusband, fearing that he would be inconvenienced by want of a watch whilst these were under repair, procured this new watch as a present. I got no fresh news from the Te-ling Kusho. He and the other officials here are waiting anxiously for the Amban's reply to the Viceroy's despatch.

In the evening Mr. Hayden returned from his trip to Ta-tsang and Tso-lamo. He was followed by the Tibetans, but not interfered with in any way.

Supplies continue to arrive daily at the Jong-chiefly fuel. Local rumour says that an enumeration has been made of all animals, the property of the villagers round about here, in order that the people shall not be able to sell to us without the knowledge of the Jongpen. That orders have been issued throughout the country by the Lhasa Government that no animals (mules, ponies, &c.) are to be taken to the Kalimpong fair this year, nor is any wool to be exported.

4th October, 1903.—Clear morning, but clouds over the Sikkim frontier. Maximum temperature 59°; minimum 34.5°.

The only news is that the Depon is starting in a day or two for his country-place near Shigatse. He requires change of air and hopes to shake off his illness in fresh surroundings.

5th October.—Bright clear morning. Some scattered clouds still on the mountains to the south. Maximum temperature 56.5°; minimum 28.4°.

I received orders to leave Khamba Jong for Darjeeling and started off my kit about noon. Captain Cullen rode over from Tangu. In the afternoon the Te-ling Kusho and the old Jongpen called, bringing back the gold watch which Colonel Younghusband had sent to the Abbot as a present for the Penchen Rinpoche. They said that the Abbot and Ba-du-la had consulted together, and had decided that, under present circumstances, it would be best not to accept the watch; as until the negotiations here had assumed a satisfactory footing, the acceptance of such a present might convey false impression to the Tibetans in general, and might lead them to harbour unjust suspicions regarding the Tashi Lama. Accordingly they returned the watch, and asked that its presentation might be deferred until a more suitable opportunity. In reply to this I said that hitherto the Tashi Lumpo people and ourselves had lived on very friendly terms at Khamba Jong-had exchanged visits and presents-and had in every respect agreed admirably. The return of the watch would certainly be regarded by Colonel Younghusband as an act indicating suspicion and scarcely of a friendly nature; and I begged them to reconsider their decision. After some argument they agreed to place my views before the Abbot and Ba-du-la, but the Te-ling Kusho objected to being the bearer of the watch a second time. So I sent my Tibetan clerk with them to return the watch, and if possible to induce them to accept it. This however they declined to do and returned it.

The Te-ling Kusho leaves here to-morrow or the next day for a short visit to his estate at Te-ling.

From Colonel F. E. Younghusband, C.I.E., Darjeeling, to the Foreign Secretary, Simla, dated the 16th October, 1903.
(Telegraphic.)

Whereabouts of two Lachung men not known. Report says they have been killed.

From the Resident in Nepal, Segowlie, to the Deputy Commissioner, Darjeeling; repeated to the Foreign Secretary, Simla, dated the 30th October, 1903.
(Telegraphic.)

Hear from Prime Minister that 500 yaks, which were to have been delivered at Tipta La Pass, have been stopped. He has now ordered these to be taken to Phallut, and will be glad if you will arrange to take delivery as soon as they arrive there. Colonel Harak Jang will give you date of their arrival. Nepalese escort with yaks will not cross frontier, only the drivers.

Letter from Colonel F. E. Younghusband, C.I.E., British Commissioner, Tibet Frontier Commission, to the Secretary to the Government of India, in the Foreign Department, dated Khamba Jong, the 24th October, 1903.

I have the honour to submit Amban's reply to His Excellency the Viceroy's letter, dated 25th August, 1903, to him, together with an English translation of the same.

Annexure.

Letter from the Chinese Amban to His Excellency the Viceroy and Governor-General of India, dated Lhasa, the 17th October, 1903.

(Translation.)

On 10th September, I had the honour to receive Your Excellency's despatch which I have read with care and attention.

I have the honour to state in reply that the Prefect Ho was appointed to act in the discussion of matters relating to the frontier, because he was versed in this question, nor was his rank a low one. Your Excellency states that you consider his rank too low. The said Prefect has applied for leave of absence owing to illness. I have, therefore, appointed Colonel Chao, Major of Chingshi (a district near Yatung), to proceed to Khamba Jong with Mr. Parr as his joint assistant, Colonel Chao is of the third official rank, with the official button of the second rank. I trust that this arrangement is in accordance with Your

Excellency's ideas on the subject.

I have now the honour to request Your Excellency to instruct Colonel Younghusband and any others concerned to act accordingly and confer with Colonel Chao and Mr. Parr.

Your Excellency states that you are apprehensive of delay in the arrival of the newly-appointed Amban, Yu, and request me to proceed to the frontier. I am bound to cherish our international friendship strenuously. I have already requested the Dalai Lama to depute a Councillor of State (Kalon) to accompany me, but the Tibetans have not yet settled this point. When the appointment of the Councillor of State has been made, I will bring him with me.

His Excellency Yu, the newly-appointed Amban, has received the Imperial Command to hasten on his journey, and should be here in two or three months' time.

I have been inducing the Tibetans to fix a date for the Councillor's departure, but this is a matter which cannot be satisfactorily arranged at a moment's notice.

In Your Excellency's despatch reference is made to the selection of winter quarters by the two officials, Messrs. Younghusband and White. I would request Your Excellency to instruct those officers not to move their present camp, as every pass in Tibet is guarded by soldiers. It would be absolutely unheard of that the British delegates should incur danger, and thereby give rise to cause for troubling the friendly relations between Great Britain and China, a matter of the utmost moment.

I have the honour to state in conclusion that my departure (for Khamba Jong) or the arrival of His Excellency Yu at his post will be communicated by despatch to Your Excellency.

Letter from Captain P. P. Kilkelly, I.M.S., Assistant Resident in Nepal, to the Secretary to the Government of India, in the Foreign Department, dated Nepal, the 1st November, 1903. (Received at India Office, 30th November, 1903.)
(Extract.)

The Prime Minister showed me a despatch received by him from Colonel Harak Jang, dated 25th October. It states that, in compliance with Colonel Younghusband's message, which reached him on the 18th October, he immediately sent off runners to try and stop the yaks which were proceeding to Khamba Jong viâ Tipta La Pass, and which were timed to reach the pass on the 21st October. As the distance was eight marches, the runners could not reach in time, and on the 21st October the yaks in two batches of 250 each reached Tipta La. The first batch crossed the pass and encamped at Phatuk at 5 p.m. The yaks were accompanied by drivers and two unarmed Nepalese officers only. At Phatuk they were met by four mounted Tibetan officers and about sixty or eighty men armed with swords and knives. These men informed the Nepalese that they could not proceed further: they then rushed in among the animals, and terrifying them with rattles, dispersed them in all directions. There is little hope that any of these will be recovered. It was dark when the occurrence took place, and the yaks are probably all looted. The second batch was opposed at Tipta La and also dispersed, but there is hope that some of these may be recovered. No oppostiion was given to the Tibetans by the Nepalese, as the latter were unarmed. On the night of the 21st October, there was a heavy fall of snow, and five Nepalese drivers were frozen to death at Tipta La Pass. Under these circumstances, Colonel Harak Jang thinks it almost impossible to deliver the yaks at Tipta La. He has written to Mr. White and to the Deputy Commissioner, Darjeeling, that arrangements may be made to take delivery of yaks at Phallut, and he is writing to Colonel Younghusband to ask him to arrange that delivery be taken by the 12th November at Phallut.

∽◦◦

From the Secretary of State for India to the Viceroy, dated the 6th November, 1903.
(Telegraphic.)

In view of the recent conduct of the Tibetans, His Majesty's Government feel that it would be impossible not to take action, and they accordingly sanction the advance of the mission to Gyangtse. They are, however, clearly of opinion that this step should not be allowed to lead to occupation or to permanent intervention in Tibetan affairs in any form. The advance should be made for the sole purpose of obtaining satisfaction, and as soon as reparation is obtained a withdrawal should be effected. While His Majesty's Government consider the proposed action to be necessary, they are not prepared to establish a permanent mission in Tibet, and the question of enforcing trade facilities in that country must be considered in the light of the decision conveyed in this telegram.

Letter from Colonel F. E. Younghusband, C.I.E., British Commissioner, Tibet Frontier Commission, to the Secretary to the Government of India, in the Foreign Department, dated Darjeeling, the 30th November, 1903. (Received at India Office, 21st December, 1903.)

Captain Parr called on me on the 28th instant, and in the course of conversation said that the Tibetans were expecting that before any advance was made into their country the British Government would make a formal declaration of their intentions. I told him that no other declaration would be made than that already made by the Viceroy to the Amban in His Excellency's letter of November 8th. In this letter it was stated that the Mission would advance to a more suitable place for negotiations, and that, as the Amban had said that the passes were guarded by Tibetan soldiers, measures were being taken to protect the Mission during the movement and to safeguard its communications with India. If the progress of the Mission was obstructed, General Macdonald would, of course, use force to clear a way for the passage of the Mission. If on the other hand no opposition was offered to the progress of the Mission, General Macdonald would not attack the Tibetans. We were prepared to fight if fighting were forced upon us. We were equally ready to negotiate if the Chinese and Tibetans would send proper delegates to negotiate with us.

Captain Parr said that the present Amban would probably reach either Khamba Jong or Chumbi in three weeks' time. I told him that the presence of the Amban alone, without fully-empowered Tibetan delegates, would be of little use; and in any case I would not be able to negotiate with him either at Khamba Jong or in Chumbi, as experience had convinced us that no negotiations would be of avail unless conducted at some centre well inside Tibet. If, however, the Amban could persuade the Tibetans of the folly of opposing the progress of the Mission and the advisability of commencing negotiations without delay, he would be acting in their best interests.

All accounts seem to show that the Tibetans are determined to fight. But I will still do what I can to secure the arrival of the Mission at Gyantse without serious opposition.

From the Viceroy to the Secretary of State for India, dated the 6th December, 1903.
(Telegraphic.)

The Tibetan General at Yatung is reported by Colonel Younghusband to have asked to be given a pledge that if the Tibetans make no attack upon us, no attack will be made by us on them. To this Colonel Younghusband has replied that we are conducting the Mission, under adequate protection, to a place better fitted for negotiations, that we are not at war with Tibet, and that, unless we are ourselves attacked, we shall not attack the Tibetans.

From the Viceroy to the Secretary of State for India, dated the 10th December, 1903.
(Telegraphic.)

A telegram, dated 7th December, has been received from Colonel Younghusband reporting that he has been informed by Mr. Ho that Major Li is being sent by the Amban with a letter in reply to mine of the 8th November, but that the Amban is unable to come in person because a Councillor has not been appointed by the Tibetans.

From the Foreign Secretary, Viceroy's Camp, Alwar, to the Chief Secretary to the Government of Bengal, and Colonel F. E. Younghusband, C.I.E., dated the 10th December, 1903. (Received at India Office, 4th January, 1904.)

In view of fact that Mission is about to advance into Tibet, and that its character and scope have been expanded by necessity of the case, it seems desirable to place personnel of the Commission on new footing; Viceroy has, therefore, decided to invest Colonel Younghusband with superior power and with the title of British Commissioner for Tibet Frontier Matters; remaining officers-namely, Messrs. White, Wilton, and Walsh-will be styled Assistants to the Commissioner, and Captain O'Connor will be Secretary to the Commissioner.

Letter from Colonel F. E. Younghusband, C.I.E., British Commissioner, Tibet Frontier Commission, to the Secretary to the Government of India, in the Foreign Department, dated Camp, Gnatong, the 10th December, 1903. (Received at India Office, 11th January, 1904.)

I have the honour to forward, for the information of the Government of India, the translation of a letter I have received from Mr. Ho.

I do not propose making any reply to it.

Letter from Prefect Ho to Colonel F. E. Younghusband, C.I.E., British Commissioner, Tibet Frontier Commission, dated Lhasa, the 24th November, 1903.

It is a long time since we last met. On 21st October, His Excellency Yü, the Amban, replied to you in a letter, the gist of which was that he was endeavouring to persuade the Tibetans to make arrangements speedily.

On 23rd November, His Excellency received a despatch from the Viceroy of India, dated 8th November. His Excellency the Viceroy there stated that Major Chao's rank was too low, that it appeared that the Tibetan Councillor of State and the Amban would be unable to arrive [at Khamba Jong] within a reasonable time, that Colonel Younghusband and his staff could not remain on at Khamba Jong, and that some other spot would be selected for discussion.

I have now been instructed by the Amban to write and inform you that His Excellency has been trying to persuade the Lhasa officials to send deputies, but their temperament is dilatory, and on this account the Amban has been unable to come [to visit you at Khamba Jong]. Also, the Amban is afraid you have been long at Khamba Jong. He is now sending Colonel Li Fu Liu, who is of the rank of Major, to proceed there and bring pressure to bear upon the Tibetan delegates with a view to discussion. Major Li is of the same rank as [Colonel] Chao, previously appointed, being of the 3rd rank and holding a button of the 2nd rank. Major Li is of no low rank, and has been transacting official business in Tibet for several years. He is well versed in Tibetan affairs, and, on arrival, will surely be able to make the Tibetan delegates discuss matters. I trust you will not change your quarters. Major Li is the bearer of a despatch from the Amban.

In selecting officials in Tibet, it is a necessary qualification that the men chosen be of worth and ability. The number of Chinese officials to draw upon in Tibet is comparatively small and not the same as in the provinces in China. The Viceroy is requested not to mind, should the rank of the officials belonging to our respective countries be unequal.

On my return to Lhasa I was sick, but am now well again. I have the honour to direct correspondence relating to the frontier question of which I am still in charge as formerly.

From the Viceroy to the Secretary of State for India, dated 13th December, 1903.
(Telegraphic.)

Colonel Younghusband telegraphs, 11th December, as follows:-

> "Difficulties in the matter of transport have been very serious. Force left for foot of pass to-day. To-morrow I join it and cross pass with it. There are no signs of serious opposition. Walsh is here and in two or three days Wilton will join me. Khambajong party were to leave that place to-day."

From the Viceroy to the Secretary of State for India, dated 13th December, 1903.
(Telegraphic.)

Colonel Younghusband, in telegram, dated 9th December, reports as follows: Information that the Tibetans are relying on Russian support, and that Russian arms have entered Tibet, has now been received from several independent sources. It may be assumed as certain that Dorjieff, who two or three years ago went on a mission to the Czar from the Dalai Lama, is at present at Lhasa; that a promise of Russian support has been given by him to the

Tibetans; and that the Tibetans believe that this promised support will be given to them.

From the Viceroy to the Secretary of State for India, dated the 15th December, 1903.
(Telegraphic.)

Colonel Younghusband's Mission reached Rinchingong on the 13th December, with escort, having crossed the Jelap La. No opposition was encountered. At Yatung the gate was left open; the meeting of the British Commission with the Tibetan and Chinese officials was friendly, although they requested him not to pass through the gate. They gave Colonel Younghusband dinner subsequently.

From the Viceroy to the Secretary of State for India, dated the 20th December, 1903.
(Telegraphic.)

Tibet. The following telegram, dated Chumbi, 17th December, has been received from Colonel Younghusband:-

"Two good and independent sources have furnished me with information to the effect that a member of the Dalai Lama's Council has been imprisoned by the National Assembly, acting probably under orders from the Dalai Lama himself, on the ground, it is alleged, that the Councillor had no right to report that the situation was serious. Resistance may be expected at Phari as the war party is now in the ascendant. Colonel Mac Donald, who arrived at Phari about the 20th December, intends, after posts have been established there, to return to Chumbi. I purpose remaining here pending the completion of our preparations for the final advance from Kalatso to Gyantse. It may be six weeks before this takes place. It will probably be the middle of February before the new Amban arrives at Gyantse."

Note from Chang Ta-jÊn to the Marquess of Lansdowne, dated Chinese Legation, London, the 22nd December, 1903. (Received December 23.)

I am desired by the Wai-wu Pu to acquaint Your Lordship that a telegram has been received from the Chinese Resident at Lhasa, stating that the two natives of Sikkim who were reported to have been put to death by the Tibetans are alive and well, but still under detention at a place named Shaung Shang, and that instructions have been given for their immediate liberation.

A Tibetan official of the name of Ko-Pa-lung has been nominated by the Amban to act as Tibetan Commissioner; and as soon as his appointment shall have been sanctioned by the Ta-lai Lama, the Amban in person, accompanied by him, will lose no time in proceeding to Ya-tung, there to meet, and negotiate with, the British Commissioner, a settlement of all pending issues.

Under these circumstances, the Wai-wu Pu hope

that it will not be considered necessary for the British forces to proceed further into Thibet.

From the Viceroy to the Secretary of State for India, dated 23rd December, 1903.
(Telegraphic.)

Younghusband telegraphs from Chumbi, under date 18th December, that the Phari Jongpen had visited him on that day, and stated that there were few troops at that place. Younghusband advised him not to resist our advance, as we were quite strong enough to force our way; and told him that we should look to him for supplies. He said that we would not be resisted and that supplies would be forthcoming. MacDonald on the same day found people at Lengmathong willing to supply as much grass as he required, and the inhabitants of the Valley are bringing in all the supplies they can, as well as sixty mules which, on the same day, were offered for sale.

From the Viceroy to the Secretary of State for India, dated the 24th December, 1903.
(Telegraphic.)

Following telegram, dated 22nd December, from Younghusband:-

"Macdonald has reached Phari without opposition, and has reconnoitred up to the Tangla Pass and found it unoccupied. During the week we have been in Chumbi the inhabitants have sold us 800 maunds grass, 56 maunds turnips, 5 maunds potatoes, 7 maunds buckwheat, and 100 mules. Walsh and Bretherton have, in addition, arranged for 400 mules to ply on contract system between here and Rowatang, on the Rungpo."

From the Viceroy to the Secretary of State for India, dated the 25th December, 1903.
(Telegraphic.)

Tibet. General Macdonald telegraphs from Phari, dated 23rd instant, that he arrived there on the 22nd; all well. There were no Tibetan troops in the place, and the jong, or fort, was only occupied by a few local officials, including the Depon. He had garrisoned the fort with 150 Gurkhas and one 7-pounder gun, and intended to leave them there with rations for 10 days. The inhabitants of the town of Phari are between 2,000 and 3,000 in number, and are friendly; there is also a considerable amount of forage and supplies. He had reconnoitered the Tang-la and the country beyond it up to a distance of 12 miles from Phari, and had found no hostile force. The Depon and local officials are staying in the fort, thus making a joint occupation with the troops. He proposed to return to new Chumbi on the morning of the 24th with the rest of his column and to arrive there the same day. The troops are bearing well the high elevation and the cold. The thermometer registered 41½ degrees of frost on the night of the 22nd.

From the Viceroy to the Secretary of State for India, dated the 31st December, 1903.
(Telegraphic.)

Colonel Younghusband telegraphs from Chumbi, 26th December, as follows:-

> "Captain Parr and Colonel Chao have been informed by the Amban that he intends to leave Lhasa to-day, and that he expects to reach Phari in three weeks' time. Yesterday, I received a visit from Colonel Chao, who requested me not to proceed beyond Phari; in reply, I have informed him that I had to move towards Lhasa and conduct negotiations in Tibet proper in order that the Tibetans might be impressed and their obstinacy overcome. I have requested General Macdonald to make arrangements for the Mission, with a sufficient escort, to leave Phari a fortnight hence, and move towards Kalatso. General Macdonald has agreed to make the necessary arrangements. Before the final advance to Gyantse can be made it may, perhaps, be necessary for us to remain for some weeks at Kalatso.

I replied to Colonel Younghusband, on the 31st:-

> "Government approve your proposed move to Kalatso. You will, of course, take steps to ensure, in regard to the march across the Tang-la and in the selection of a suitable locality for the halt which you propose to make on the far side of the pass, that all necessary precautions are taken."

From the Viceroy to the Secretary of State for India, dated 2nd January, 1904.
(Telegraphic.)

Colonel Younghusband telegraphs, on the 29th December, as follows:-

"In the course of informal conversation to-day, Colonel Chao stated that Dorjieff is at present in Lhasa. He also said that the arrogance of the Tibetans was due to their reliance on the support of the Russians, since many discussions have been held in Russia between Dorjieff and Russian officials with the result that of late the Tibetans have been taunting the Chinese openly and saying that they have now a stronger and greater Power than China upon which to rely for assistance."

From the Viceroy to the Secretary of State for India, dated 3rd January, 1904.
(Telegraphic.)

The following telegram, dated New Chumbi, the 30th December, has been received from General MacDonald:-

"I am making arrangements for the advance of the Mission 17 miles beyond Phari to Thuna. The Mission, accompanied by a flying column, will leave here on 4th January and on the 8th will arrive at Thuna, at which place it will remain with an escort composed of four companies of

the 23rd Pioneers, the 8th Gurkhas, the British
Machine Gun Section, one seven-pounder gun,
and Medical, Supply, and Sapper detachments.
After the Mission has been established at Thuna,
I shall return to Phari and, if necessary, to
Chumbi, taking with me the remainder of the
troops forming the flying column, to allow of the
collection at Phari of supplies sufficient for a
further advance. The weather is still fine. Reports
from Phari state that all is well there and mention
the arrival of a few Lamas and Chinese officials
from Lhasa. Major Ray, who joined on the 29th
December, has been appointed officiating Deputy
Assistant Quartermaster-General to the force."

*Letter from Colonel F. E. Younghusband, C.I.E., British
Commissioner for Tibet Frontier Matters, to the Secretary to
the Government of India in the Foreign Department, dated
Chumbi (Tibet), 31st December, 1903. (Received at India
Office, 25th January, 1904.)*

I have on more than one occasion expressed my conviction that the opposition of the Tibetans to
intercourse with us comes from the Lhasa authorities,
and that the people themselves are perfectly ready to
have dealings with us. I have just had absolute proof
that this is the case.

From the first day that we entered this valley the
people have sold supplies to the Commissariat; in each
camp even women may be seen bringing in eggs, butter, and milk to sell to the sepoys individually, and any

day now numbers of coolies may be seen descending into the valley from the Sikkim side carrying loads of cigarettes and little luxuries which the traders of Chumbi have ordered over to sell to the troops.

But since our arrival one high lay and three high ecclesiastical authorities from Lhasa have reached Phari, and have at once forbidden the inhabitants to sell us anything-even wood. And this action has been taken, though Colonel Chao, whose permanent post is Commandant at Phari, and who is for the time being the representative of the Chinese Government, assured me yesterday that he had given orders at Phari that everything was to be supplied us, as we paid liberally for what we got.

Such action, moreover, is only a counterpart of what took place at Khamba Jong. There were thousands of sheep there; the people were anxious to make money by selling them at a good price to us: the local official was no less anxious to derive a little pecuniary advantage from the transaction. Colonel Chao also promised Mr. Wilton-and sincerely as Mr. Wilton thinks-to see the sheep provided for us, but only a few were forthcoming, and Colonel Chao told me yesterday that the reason was that the Lhasa representative had absolutely forbidden the people to sell them.

This being the policy of the Lhasa authorities, and the provision of supplies being a necessity to us, and of no harm but of only advantage to the people, I am insisting that the people shall not be prevented from dealing with us.

From the Viceroy to the Secretary of State for India, dated 4th January, 1904.
(Telegraphic.)

I have received a telegram from Colonel Younghusband in which he reports his plans. As at present advised, he intends to leave Chumbi on the 4th January, and to proceed beyond Tungla to Thuna, where he expects to arrive on the 8th January. A halt for one week will be made at Thuna; the Mission will then advance to Kalatso and remain there for some three weeks. It is expected that by the middle of February Gyantse will be reached.

From the Viceroy to the Secretary of State for India, dated 11th January, 1904.
(Telegraphic.)

Colonel Younghusband telegraphs from Phari on the 8th January as follows:-

"I arrived here on the 6th January. The attitude of three high Lhasa monks is most unfriendly. They refuse to come and see us and prevent the people, who are friendly, from selling things. The Chinese officials are also professedly friendly. It is reported that the Amban is experiencing difficulty in obtaining transport from the Tibetans and is being detained in consequence. No snow has fallen; in the day time it is warm, the sun shining brightly. At night the temperature is 7° below zero.

Letter from Colonel F. E. Younghusband, C.I.E., British Commissioner for Tibet Frontier Matters, to the Secretary to the Government of India, in the Foreign Department, dated Camp Thuna, the 11th January, 1904. (Received at India Office 13th February, 1904.)
(Extract.)

The general attitude of the Tibetans has lately become distinctly unfavourable. Before I left Chumbi reports had reached me that the representatives of the three great Lhasa monasteries and the Depon (General), who had recently arrived at Phari from Lhasa, were intimidating the people, and preventing them from selling supplies or hiring out transport to us, and I spoke to Colonel Chao about this, and asked him to see that the people were not prevented from dealing with us. Colonel Chao readily consented to do this, but frankly acknowledged that he had little power over the Tibetans. He said that at Khamba Jong he had tried his best to get supplies for us, but the Lhasa officials had thwarted him; and he went on to say that the Tibetans had during the last few months assumed a most truculent attitude and openly taunted the Chinese with their weakness, and assured them they no longer looked to them for protection, but looked instead to the Russians. On my arrival at Phari, General Macdonald told me that Major Rowe, who commands the detachment there, had reported to him many cases in which the inhabitants had expressed their willingness to deal with us, but feared to do so on account of the threats of the Lhasa functionaries. Our experience all the way through Chumbi, and even at Phari before the arrival of these Lhasa men, had been that the inhabitants were most anxious to make money from dealing with us. There was not, therefore, any doubt that the Lhasa monks deliberately put obstacles in our way, and prevented the people from reaping the benefit of our presence. I accordingly sent Captain O'Connor to see the Lhasa men-who, it may be remarked, made no sign of visiting me-and to ask them to come and see General Macdonald and discuss the question of supplies and transport for the troops with him. They absolutely refused to come, and denied that they had prevented the people from dealing with us. Captain O'Connor reported that the three monks were exceedingly surly, and said they would discuss nothing whatever until we went back to Yatung. Shortly after Captain O'Connor's return, Major Li, who had been deputed by the Amban to take Colonel Chao's place on the Commission, came to visit me, and I told him of the surprise with which I had found Colonel Chao's orders that the Phari people should be allowed to sell us supplies had been thwarted by the Lhasa monks. I informed him that they had refused to come and see General Macdonald, and I asked him, therefore, to take action to see that Colonel Chao's orders were given effect to. He said he would write at once to the Lhasa officials, and get from them an assurance that they would not prevent the people selling. But he also, like Colonel Chao, said they were a most obstinate people, and at present would pay no respect to the Chinese, as they were so fully relying on Russian support. Captain O'Connor tells me that the whole demeanour of these Lhasa monks-who are the men who really guide the destinies of Tibet-was impracticable in the extreme. They made no advance in civility, though I instructed Captain O'Connor to be studiously polite in his behaviour, and they adopted the high tone of demanding our withdrawal to Yatung before any discussion could take place. All I asked of them was an assurance that they would not prevent willing people from selling supplies to us, and even this little they refused both the Chinese and me. The worst feature of the situation is, though, that the local people and even the Chinese think that in advancing into Tibet we are advancing to our destruction. They are not impressed by our troops; they know how few they are; they know of thousands of Tibetan troops on this side of the pass; and they believe that these new Lhasa-made rifles and the new drill will prevent them from incurring the loss they did in the last campaign against us. Numbers of our camp followers deserted, and local men in our employ all brought in stories of the numbers and prowess of the Tibetans, and how they intended to attack us in the night and swamp us. We have, in fact, as I have so often remarked, not one ounce of prestige on this frontier. I have, therefore, nothing to work with in making a settlement. Rather than being afraid of us, the Tibetans up here in Tibet think we ought to be afraid of them, and the retirement from Khamba Jong, has, I fear, done much to convince them that we are.

From the Viceroy to the Secretary of State for India, dated 12th January, 1904.
(Telegraphic.)

From telegraphic information which I have received, it appears that the Tibet Mission left Phari on the 7th instant, accompanied by the escort, crossed Tangla Pass, and on the 8th arrived at Thuna, which is situated 17 miles from Phari. On the same day three Lhasa lamas, who had been at Phari, left that place, together with the local Depon. As this official was taking his departure, a slight fracas occurred, some stones-one of which injured Lieutenant Grant, of the 8th Ghurkas-being thrown. The injured officer, however, is doing well. In a report from Colonel Younghusband, dated Thuna, the 10th January, it is stated that the mounted infantry have located a camp of 2,000 Tibetans at a spot 10 miles to the north-west of Thuna. Colonel Younghusband says he will make every effort to bring about a settlement by peaceful means, but he sees no chance of a settlement being effected until the power of the monks at Lhasa is broken, so complete is the reliance of the Tibetans on the support of Russia and so hostile is their whole attitude.

From the Viceroy to the Secretary of State for India, dated 14th January, 1904.
(Telegraphic.)

A report received from General Macdonald, dated Phari, the 11th January, states that he left the Mission

in Thuna and returned to Phari on the 11th. The
Mission was occupying a strong position in a walled
enclosure which contained a well and some houses.
All the supplies available were left for their use. The
following troops remained at Thuna as escort, under
command of Lieutenant-Colonel Hogge:-

Four companies of the 23rd Pioneers.

One section Norfolk Regiment.

20 Madras Sappers.

1 machine gun.

1 7-pounder.

Supply and Medical detachments.

An intimation was received from the Tibetans to
the effect that unless the Mission moved forward to
Kalatso no hostilities were intended. Colonel
Younghusband is remaining at Thuna for political reasons. No casualties have occurred among the men,
although both the troops and the animals have found
the severe cold and the strong winds trying.

*Letter from Colonel F. E. Younghusband, C.I.E., British
Commissioner for Tibet Frontier Matters, to the Secretary to
the Government of India, in the Foreign Department, dated
Camp Thuna (Tibet) the 15th January, 1904. (Received at
India Office, 13th February, 1904.)*
(Extract.)

In continuation of my telegram of yesterday's date, I
have the honour to make the following more detailed
report of my visit to the Tibetan Chiefs at Guru.
Though I had every right to expect that they should

visit me here, and when they demanded that I should go out to meet them half-way, I refused, yet I did not wish to lose any opportunity of influencing them on the one hand and of gaining first-hand knowledge of them on the other. I wished specially to see them and judge of them in their own natural surroundings. I, therefore, determined, without any formality and without previous announcement, to ride over to their camp and talk over the general situation, not as the British Commissioner with a list of grievances for which he had to demand redress, but as one who wished to understand them and seek by friendly means to effect a settlement. I was only too well aware that such an attempt was likely to be mistaken by the Tibetans as a sign of weakness, still when I see these people so steeped in ignorance of what opposing the might of the British Empire really means, I feel it my duty to reason with them up to the latest moment to save them from the results of their ignorance. I was accompanied by Captain O'Connor and by Captain Sawyer of the 23rd Pioneers, but by no one else. On our way we were met by the messengers who had come to say the Tibetan Chiefs would not come to see me at Thuna. I was all the more pleased, then, that I had left Thuna before the message arrived. On reaching Guru, a small village under a hill, we found numbers of Tibetan soldiers out collecting yak-dung in the surrounding plain, but there was no military precaution whatever taken. About 600 soldiers were huddled up in tents in the cattle-yards of the village, without any defence, and a company of infantry

might go out from here at any time, and by occupying the height above the village, annihilate the whole
Tibetan force, for they are only armed with
matchlocks and spears and have no breech-loaders. As
we rode through the village, the soldiers all crowded
out to look at us, laughing and smiling and with no
ugly looks. They were not very different in appearance from the ordinary Bhutia dandy-bearer one sees
at Darjeeling, or the yak-driver of this country. On
reaching the principal house, I was received at the
head of the stairs by the Tibetan General, who was
very polite and cordial in his greeting. Other Generals
stood behind him, and smiled and shook hands also. I
was then conducted into a room in which the three
Lhasa monks were seated. They made no attempt to
rise, and only made a barely civil salutation from their
cushions. The Lhasa General and Shigatse General
took their seats on cushions at the head of the room
opposite the monks. We were given three cushions on
the right, and two Shigatse Generals and another
Shigatse representative had seats on the left. Tea was
served, and the Lhasa General, as the spokesman of
the assembly, asked after my health. After suitable
inquiries on my part, I said that, though they had not
come to see me either at Phari or here, and I could
not pay them a formal visit as British Commissioner,
and had not in any case any intention of officially discussing the various points of difference between us,
yet I was anxious to see them and know them, and to
have an opportunity of freely discussing the general
situation in a friendly informal way, so I had ridden

over without ceremony and without escort, in my private capacity, to talk matters over with them, and see if there was no way of arriving at a settlement by peaceful means. I said I had been appointed British Commissioner on account of my general experience in many different countries; that I had no preconceived ideas upon the question, or no animus against the Tibetans; that from what I had seen of them I was convinced there was no people with whom we were more likely to get on with than with them, and I hoped now we had really met each other face to face we should find a means of settling our differences and forming a lasting friendship. The Lhasa General replied that all the people of Tibet had a covenant that no Europeans were ever to be allowed to enter their country, and the reason was that they wished to preserve their religion. The monks here chimed in that the religion must be preserved, and no European on any account allowed in Tibet, and the General went on to say that, if I really wanted to make a friendly settlement, I should go back to Yatung. I told him that for 150 years we had remained quietly in India and made no attempt to force ourselves upon them. Even though we had a treaty right to station a Political Officer at Yatung, we had not exercised that right. But of recent years we had heard from many different sources that they were entering into friendly relations with the Russians, while they were still keeping us at arm's length. One Dorjieff, for instance, had been the bearer of autograph letters from the Dalai Lama to the Czar and his officials at the very time when the

Dalai Lama had refused letters from the Viceroy of India. We could understand their being friendly with both the Russians and us or being unfriendly with both; but when they were friendly with the Russians and unfriendly with us, they must not be surprised at our now paying closer attention to the assertion of our treaty rights. The General assured me that it was untrue that they had any dealings with the Russians, and the monks brusquely intimated that they disliked them just as much as they did us. They protested that they had nothing to do with the Russians; that there was no Russian near Lhasa at the present time; and that Dorjieff was a Mongolian, and the custom of Mongolians was to make large presents to the monasteries; and they asked me not to be so suspicious. I said it was difficult not to be suspicious when they persistently kept us at such a distance. I then addressed them in regard to religion, and asked them if they had ever heard that we interfered with the religions of the people of India. They admitted that we did not, but they maintained that, nevertheless, it was to preserve their religion that they adhered to their determination to keep us out. As the Buddhist religion nowhere preaches this seclusion, it is evident that what the monks wish to preserve is not their religion, but priestly influence. So far, the conversation, in spite of occasional bursts from the monks, had been maintained with perfect good humour, but when I made sign of going and said that I hoped they would come and see me at Thuna, their tone suddenly changed and they said we must go back to Yatung. One of the

Generals said-though with perfect politeness of man-
ner-that we had broken the rule of the road in
coming into their country, and that we were nothing
but thieves and brigands in occupying Phari fort. The
monks, using forms of speech generally addressed to
inferiors, loudly clamoured for me to name a date for
our retirement from Thuna before I left the room; the
atmosphere became electric; the faces of all became
set; a General left the room; trumpets outside were
sounded and attendants closed round us. It was necessary to keep extremely cool under these
circumstances. I said that I would have to obey whatever orders I received from my Government just as
they had to obey orders from theirs; that I would ask
them to report to their Government what I had said,
and I would report to my Government what they had
told me-that was all that could be done at present.
The monks continued to clamour for me to name a
date, but a General relieved the situation by suggest-
ing that a messenger should return with me to Thuna
to receive my answer there. The other Generals
accepted the suggestion, and the tension was
removed. Their faces became smiling again, and they
conducted me to the outer door with the same
geniality and politeness with which they had received
us, though the monks remained seated and as surly
and evil-looking as men well could be. The messengers have arrived at Thuna, and as a convoy with
escort has also arrived, I have sent back a message to
say that I have received orders to proceed on into
Tibet. This my first meeting with really representative

Tibetans after six months' waiting has led to no result as far as persuading them to any more reasonable attitude goes. But it has given me the opportunity I had long been wanting of absolutely assuring myself of the real attitude of the various parties in the State. My conclusions are that the monks are implacably hostile; that they have the preponderating influence in the State; that they are entirely convinced of their power to dictate to us and ignorant of their weakness; that the lay officials are much less unfriendly and more amenable to influence and less ignorant of our strength; that the military organisation is quite contemptible; and that the ordinary people and soldiers, though perhaps liable to be worked on by the monks, have no innate bad feeling against us. The desire of the monks to preserve their priestly influence is our only real obstacle.

From the Viceroy to the Secretary of State for India, dated 16th January, 1904.
(Telegraphic.)

I have received a report from Colonel Younghusband at Thuna, in which he states that the villagers are friendly and supplies are being furnished by them, although there are rumours of opposition ahead. A message was received on the 12th January from the Depon and the Lhasa officials requesting an interview with Colonel Younghusband. At noon, which was the hour fixed by Colonel Younghusband for the reception of the deputation, several hundred men appeared on the plain below the village. Colonel Younghusband, in reply to a message from the Tibetans asking him to meet them half way, said that they were welcome at any time at his camp if they desired to see him.

From the Viceroy to the Secretary of State for India, dated 17th January, 1904.
(Telegraphic.)

Colonel Younghusband telegraphs, on the 13th instant, from Thuna, as follows:-

"In compliance with a request made by the emissaries from Lhasa that I would go out to meet them I deputed Captain O'Connor to do so. The Lhasa officials, after they had once more urged us to return to Yatung, eventually stated that they were prepared to discuss matters here at Thuna. This constitutes a distinct improvement upon the attitude adopted by them at Phari, and their general demeanour was much more cordial, according to Captain O'Connor's report. The camp on our flank has retired, and the Lhasa officials have returned to Guru, six miles down the valley, accompanied by the whole of their following. They told Captain O'Connor that, if we advanced and they were defeated they would fall back upon another Power and that things would then be bad for us. In the course of conversation with the Munshi they told him that they would prevent us from advancing beyond our present position; they also repudiated the Sikkim Convention and said that they were tired of the Chinese and were quite capable of concluding a treaty by themselves."

From the Viceroy to the Secretary of State for India, dated 20th January, 1904.
(Telegraphic.)

The following report, dated Thuna, the 14th January, has been received from Colonel Younghusband:-

"On the 13th January I paid an unceremonial visit to the Tibetans at Guru, six miles further down the valley, in order that by informal discussion I might assure myself of their real attitude. O'Connor and Sawyer accompanied me. There were present at the interview three monks and one general from Lhasa, as well as three generals and another delegate from Shigatse. These, since the Councillors have been deposed, are the leading men in Tibet, and they form the most representative body of Tibetans ever met by Europeans. The general from Lhasa acted as spokesman, but the ruling influence was possessed by the monks, who clamoured loudly for the withdrawal of the Mission to Yatung, declaring that for the preservation of their religion-by which they probably meant their priestly influence-no European could be allowed by them in Tibet. These monks were low-bred persons, insolent, rude, and intensely hostile; the generals, on the other hand, were polite and well-bred. Some 600 soldiers, armed with spears and matchlocks (no breech-loaders being visible) were present-affable, grinning yokels of the yak-driver type. There was a complete absence of defences, and of military precautions of any sort, although the place was a death-trap where the Tibetans could have been annihilated by a single company. It seemed to me that the generals had no nerve, and stood in greater fear of their own people than of us; they did not affect to have any regard for the Amban, and had received no information as to the probable date of his arrival."

Letter from Colonel F. E. Younghusband, C.I.E., British Commissioner for Tibet Frontier Matters, to the Secretary to the Government of India in the Foreign Department, dated Camp Thuna, the 22nd January, 1904. (Recieved at India Office 20th February, 1904.)
(Extract.)

As I had the honour to report in my telegram of yesterday, the Lhasa General, known as the Lhi-ding Depon, visited me yesterday in company with a high Shigatse official and the Depon of the Chumbi valley who had met me at Yatung. The Lhasa General announced that, like me, he was most anxious to come to a friendly settlement, and, therefore, he would ask me to withdraw to Yatung where discussions could then take place in the most amicable manner. I told him I did not wish to say anything disagreeable to himself personally, as he had always been polite to me, but I would ask him to let his Government know that the time was past for talk of this kind, and to warn them that they must take a more serious view of the situation. They must realise that the British Government were exceedingly angry at the treatment that I, their representative, had received, and were in no mood to be trifled with. Far from going back or even staying here, we were going to advance still further into Tibet: and I expected to be met both by the Amban and by a Tibetan official of the highest rank who would have sufficient authority to negotiate a proper treaty with me in the place of the one concluded by the Amban, which the Tibetans repudiated. I had waited for six months for a proper representative to be sent to meet me, but even now none had arrived. The Lhasa General said that, if we went back to the frontier, all could be arranged, but that if we went on there would be trouble. I told him we were not afraid of trouble: that I had brought with me only a few soldiers now, but if trouble arose, there were thousands more who could follow after. I did not wish to say this in a threatening way, but that he might warn his Government that we are thoroughly in earnest. I claimed we had advanced in a reasonably friendly manner and had paid liberally for every ounce of grain, every blade of grass, and every pony, mule or yak we had taken and given handsome rent for every house we had occupied. The Lhasa General said he would report what I had said to the Lhasa monks at Guru and would communicate with me again. He maintained, when I told him that neither the Amban nor the Dalai Lama had informed me of any high Tibetan official having been appointed to meet me, that he and the Lhasa monks had been specially deputed to meet me and negotiate with me, but only at Yatung. I told him that while I was quite ready to talk over matters in an informal manner with him, as I had done, I of course could only enter into regular negotiations with men with proper credentials. The conversation then became general, and I asked why it was that while Tibetans went down to India without hindrance, travelled there as long and as far as they liked, traded there, resided there, and saw their sacred places duly respected and protected by us, not a single Englishman or native of India was allowed into Tibet. This did not appear to me either a very hospitable or a very fair arrangement. What was the reason of it? The General said the reason was the difference in religion. I told him I could not accept that, for I had carefully studied their religion and found that it inculcated the brotherhood of man, and hospitality and generosity to strangers–not exclusiveness. The General then said that the Tibetans were the "inner" people, implying that they were above the rules applicable to the rest of the world. I asked him if he would do me the favour to have their sacred books searched and send me any text sanctioning inhospitality to strangers. He replied that there was no text sanctioning exclusion, but that there was an agreement or covenant of the whole people that strangers should not be admitted to Tibet. I said in that case the matter was very simple: if there was no divine command that strangers should be excluded, but merely an agreement of the people all that had to be done now was for the people to make a fresh agreement more in accordance with the spirit of their religion and admitting instead of excluding strangers. The General laughed at this, but said that the agreement once having been made could not be altered. I told him I could understand a disagreeable people wishing to keep to themselves. What was so aggravating was that a pleasant and genial people like the Tibetans wishing to debar the rest of the world from the pleasure of their society. The Lhasa General looks very well bred, he has good manners, and speaks well. But he is not clever, he has little strength of character, and he is absolutely in the hands of his three monk colleagues.

From the Viceroy to the Secretary of State for India, dated 25th January, 1904.
(Telegraphic.)

Colonel Younghusband telegraphs from Thuna on the 21st January as follows:-

"I received to-day a visit from the General from Lhasa. He stated that, though he was most anxious to effect settlement amicably, it was necessary for the Mission first to return to Yatung. In reply to this I said that I must give him a friendly warning that the time for talk like this had passed; that the Mission, so far from going back, intended to go forward; and that I would ask him to urge upon his Government the advisability of taking a more serious view of the situation. The General replied that there would be trouble if the Mission went forward, and that he himself was unable to make any report to his Government except from Yatung. I informed him that, though we too were anxious to effect a settlement without trouble if possible, yet that we were not afraid of trouble. The General promised to communicate with me again after he had informed the monks from Lhasa, who are at Guru, of the tenour of my reply. It is clear that the Lhasa General is the representative of the moderate party; the monks, however, who are irreconcilable, overweigh him. Good temper prevailed throughout the interview."

From the Viceroy to the Secretary of State for India, dated 27th January, 1904.
(Telegraphic.)

Colonel Younghusband telegraphs, on the 23rd January, from Thuna, as follows:-
"I learn from Captain Parr, who is of opinion that the Tibetans mean to make a stand at Kalatso, that the Dalai Lama has informed the Amban that the Tibetans intend to fight, and, further, that he does not intend to give the Amban an opportunity of selling Tibet to the British. Captain Parr also states that the Amban has been prevented from proceeding to meet me by the Tibetans."

From the Viceroy to the Secretary of State for India, dated 28th January, 1904.
(Telegraphic.)

In a telegram dated Chumbi, the 27th January, General Macdonald reports as follows:-

"I learn from information received from Thuna that reinforcements, consisting of cavalry, infantry and a few guns, have reached the Tibetans at Guru, who are threatening trouble if the escort and the Mission refuse to withdraw. This news is corroborated by bazaar rumours from Phari. It is possible that before long an attack may be made upon the Mission, as reports have been received that further reinforcements, from Shigatse and from Lhasa, are on their way. Colonel Younghusband and Lieutenant-Colonel Hogge; of the 23rd Pioneers, Commanding the escort at Thuna, are quite confident that their position is secure. I am, however, holding myself in readiness to move to their support, at short notice, with a column of 1,000 men and three guns. In the meantime, the work of pushing on supplies to Phari and of improving the roads is proceeding. The weather looks more threatening and there has been slight snow on the passes."

From the Secretary of State for India to the Viceroy, dated 30th January, 1904.

Your telegram 28th January. Every safeguard should

be employed to ensure security of Mission, but Colonel Younghusband should be definitely instructed to observe the spirit of his statement to the Tibetan General, reported in your telegram of the 6th December. No hostile action must be taken by him unless he is attacked or finds that there is actual danger of his communications with base being cut off by Tibetans.

From the Viceroy to the Secretary of State for India, dated the 4th February, 1904.
(Telegraphic.)

I have received a telegram from Colonel Younghusband, dated Thuna, the 31st January, in which he describes the present situation as follows:-

"All authority has been taken by the Dalai Lama into his own hands. He has ignored the Chinese, has thrown his Councillors into prison, and has defied us. His confidence in his ability to maintain the traditional policy of keeping us absolutely at arm's length and in his power to remove us from Tibet is complete. Officials and people share this confidence in the strength of Tibet and the impotence of the British Government. In consequence of this feeling, the monks and generals sent from Lhasa as delegates by the Dalai Lama refused with supreme superciliousness to negotiate at any other place than Yatung, and demanded our withdrawal from Thuna with insolent assurance. At the same time

I am unable to detect on the part of the people as a whole any sign of national opposition to us. Even the officials display great indifference, while the common people are perfectly friendly. The real opposition we are encountering is that of the Dalai Lama and his followers, the monks at Lhasa, who declare that they are concerned for the preservation of their religion, in other words, of their priestly influence by which the Tibetans are at present strangled. The influence of the Chinese has vanished completely, the present weak Amban being confronted with a young and headstrong Dalai Lama; nor is it likely to be revived when the new Amban arrives at Lhasa (which he is expected to do within the next few days) as he is not supported by Chinese troops. To influence the Dalai Lama, therefore, we must rely on our own efforts. Advance is necessary, at least as far as Gyangtse; but I am informed by General Macdonald that it will be the middle of March before this can take place. Opposition is probable when we reach Kalatso but it cannot be serious, as the Tibetan soldiers are so poorly armed, and their generals are so devoid of military experience and so lacking in nerve. It is possible that the Tibetans may be more amenable upon our arrival at Gyangtse when they have realised how powerless they are to resist our advance. Except for the Madras Sappers and Miners who were sent back yesterday the health of the troops is good, although Thuna is 15,019 feet above sea level and the minimum temperature recorded is-16. The worst month is now over. The Tibetan Camp upon our flank has been precipitately evacuated by its occupants, and our dak and convoy now pass without hindrance between this place and Phari. Grass sufficient for some weeks to come and any quantity of fuel are obtainable."

I had an interview yesterday with the Prime Minister of Nepal. He too informed me that the Tibetans were determined to oppose the Mission; and he expressed the opinion that we might be compelled to advance to Lhasa to conclude a treaty, unless the Tibetans made an attack upon us and received severe punishment, in which case they might be willing to negotiate at Gyangtse.

From Brigadier-General J. R. L. Macdonald, C.B., Chumbi, to the Adjutant-General in India, dated the 6th February, 1904. (Received at India Office 29th February, 1904.) (Telegraphic.)

All reported quiet at Thuna and Phari. Tibetans reported to be sending men back to Gyangtse from Guru for food. Snow fell on three consecutive days at Thuna, stopping work one day. The telegraph cut near Phari village fined 400 maunds yak-dung. Telegraph detachment has had 14 cases frost-bite from drifting snow and high wind.

From Brigadier-General J. R. L. Macdonald, C.B., Phari

Jong, to the Adjutant-General in India; repeated to the
Foreign Secretary, Calcutta, dated the 10th February, 1904.
(Received at India Office 5th March, 1904.)
(Telegraphic.)

Phari, tenth. Am moving over to-morrow to Thuna
with large convoy of month's supplies and fuel for
garrison at Thuna, and return here on twelfth.
Colonel Younghusband also returns here with me on
twelfth to interview the Tongsa Penlop expected here
from Bhutan.

Letter from E. H. C. Walsh, Esq., Assistant to the British
Commissioner for Tibet Frontier Matters, to Colonel F. E.
Younghusband, C.I.E., British Commissioner for Tibet
Frontier Matters, dated Phari Fort, the 25th February,
1904. (Received at India Office 28th March, 1904).
(Extract.)

I have the honour to report, for your information, the
results of an interview which the Timpuk Jongpen
had with me this morning. I received him, as on the
two previous occasions, in a tent which I had pitched
for the purpose on the plain about three hundred
yards from the fort. A guard-of-honour of half a company of the 8th Gurkhas were also in attendance as on
the previous occasions. After exchange of compliments, the Timpuk Jongpen referred to the copy of
the Kah-gyur or Buddhist Canon of Scripture, consisting of one hundred volumes, which is kept in the
Lha-Khang or Chapel of the Phari Fort, and asked if

he might be allowed to buy if for a new monastery he was building at Timpuk, or, if that was not approved, that he might be allowed to remove it to the Chatsa monastery for its safe custody to prevent its being removed or damaged by the soldiers. I informed him that we could not sell the Kah-gyur to any one, as we were only occupying the fort as a matter of necessity, and that we had not taken the Kah-gyur for ourselves, but were keeping it carefully for those to whom it belonged. I informed him that I had already inspected it to see that all the volumes were there in their racks, and that no one had interfered with it in any way, and that strict orders had been issued that no one was to meddle with it. He thanked me for this, and further asked that the Lha-Khang might not be occupied by soldiers; as in addition to the volumes of the Kah-gyur, it contained the Chapel altar with four images, which they might damage. I informed him that the room was only used as a hospital for the sick, for which it had been selected as being the only room large enough and suitable, and that as this was a work of mercy, I felt sure that he would agree with me that this was not an unsuitable purpose to use the Chapel for, and that the soldiers in hospital were always under supervision, and had strict orders not to touch the altar or its images, or the books in the racks on the wall on either side of it. I told him that the English never interfered with other people's religion, and mentioned the trouble which the English had taken to find out the birthplace of Buddha at Kapilavastu. I also told him how carefully the temple of Buddha at

Gaya was preserved. He thanked me for the assurance that no damage should be done to the books or to the images. I then informed him that the Bhutanese were already bringing in stores from Bhutan for sale to the Commissariats, and asked if he would assist in obtaining further supplies. He said he would be very pleased to do so, and would issue orders that all supplies from Bhutan that came into Tibet are to be offered for sale to the Commissariats, through Ugyen Kazi, the agent for Bhutan, whom he wished on be entrusted with this duty. I thanked him for this assistance. I then said that I would pay him a visit at Chatsa monastery to see that he was comfortable there. He was very pleased at this, but asked me not to come to-morrow as it is an unlucky day. So I told him that I would pay him a visit on Sunday.

From the British Commissioner for Tibet Frontier Matters, Phari Jong, to the Foreign Secretary, Calcutta, dated the 1st March, 1904. (Received at India Office, 28th March, 1904.) (Telegraphic.)

Thuna, 1st March. Situation unchanged. Neither Tibetans nor Chinese show any signs of negotiations. Weather much improved, though maximum temperature still falls to plus eight. Persistent rumours of attack on us to-morrow, but as it is night of full moon, nothing to fear. Origin of rumour is probably arrival of Tibetan reinforcements below Guru.

From the British Commissioner for Tibet Frontier Matters,

Phari Jong (Tibet), to the Foreign Secretary, Calcutta, dated the 3rd March, 1904. (Received at India Office 28th March, 1904.)
(Telegraphic.)

Thuna, 3rd March. Some specially high Lamas from Lhasa have visited Guru and cursed Mission camp for five days, but reconnaissance shows no increase in number of troops there.

From the Foreign Secretary, Calcutta, to the British Commissioner for Tibet Frontier Matters, Phari Jong, dated the 9th March, 1904. (Received at India Office, 5th April, 1904.)
(Telegraphic.)

Please refer to Walsh's letter to you, dated 25th February. Government of India consider that arrangements should, if possible, be made to evacuate the chapel in the Phari Fort and locate the hospital elsewhere.

From E. H. C. Walsh, Esq., Phari Jong, to the Foreign Secretary, Calcutta, dated the 10th March, 1904. (Received at India Office 5th April, 1904.)
(Telegraphic.)

Your telegram 9th March. Have informed Officer Commanding. Arrangements are being made to evacuate chapel in Phari Fort and remove hospital elsewhere.

From Brigadier-General J. R. L. Macdonald, Chumbi (Sikkim), to the Adjutant-General in India, dated the 11th March, 1904. (Received at India Office 5th April.)
(Telegraphic.)

A fire occurred yesterday at Rorotang, destroying the post there and about 3,000 maunds supplies and forage, said to have been caused by lightning; enquiry being held. Very heavy snowstorm yesterday lasting nine hours. One foot of snow at Langram, Rinchengong, and Chumbi. Severe blizzard and four feet of snow reported from Gautsa and higher up the valley. Minimum temperature last night here plus one; Gautsa minus one.

From Brigadier-General J. R. L. Macdonald, C.B., Chumbi, to the Adjutant-General in India, dated the 14th March, 1904. (Received at India Office 9th April, 1904.)
(Telegraphic.)

Snow continues. Passes closed for men and animals for the first time. Convoy with supplies and wood for one month reached Thuna 12th, and returned safely Phari 13th in spite of snow.

From Brigadier-General Macdonald, Chumbi (Sikkim), to the Adjutant-General in India, dated the 18th March, 1904. (Received at India Office 9th April, 1904.)
(Telegraphic.)

First company mounted infantry left Linganathang to-day for Phari, second company mounted infantry arrived Chumbi from Siliguri. Arrival of ekkas over the Nathu La being much impeded by landslips caused by snow-storms. One ekka driver and one cooly killed falling over the Khud. Half brigade cooly corps left Gnatong for Chumbi.

From the Foreign Secretary, Calcutta, to the British Commissioner for Tibet Frontier Matters, Thuna, dated the 19th March, 1904. (Received at India Office 9th April, 1904.)
(Telegraphic.)

Your proposal to advance is approved and authority has been given to General Macdonald either to move at once or to delay for a week if by so doing he can secure more transport and better weather. You can arrange actual date with him. You should now write to new Amban Yutai saying that you are glad to hear of his safe arrival and trust that he is ready to settle all matters in dispute in accordance with the orders issued by Waiwupu in December, 1902, and with his own statements to Townley in January, 1903, when he said that he hoped to enlighten the Tibetans. You are therefore moving to Gyangtse to commence negotiations and hoped to meet him there and that he will secure the attendance of fully-empowered Tibetan representatives of suitable rank. The Tibetans should be warned by him that the consequences of resistance to the passage of the Mission would be very serious.

From General J. R. L. Macdonald, C.B., Chumbi, to the

Adjutant-General in India, dated the 20th March, 1904.
(Received at India Office 9th April, 1904.)
(Telegraphic.)

The second company mounted infantry proceeded yesterday to Lingmathang. Five hundred brigade coolies and three troops mules arrived at Chumbi yesterday from communications. Thirty-six ekkas should cross Natula to-day and arrive here to-morrow. Smart fall of snow last evening for about two hours.

From the Viceroy to the Secretary of State for India, dated the 27th March, 1904.
(Telegraphic.)

Colonel Younghusband reports that he has received information from Chinese official that there is no unusual gathering at Lhasa or Gyangtse, and that the number of armed Tibetans available between Thuna and Kalatso is less than 3,000. The Amban is endeavouring to come to meet Colonel Younghusband, but he is having difficulty with the Dalai Lama.

From the Viceroy to the Secretary of State for India, dated the 31st March, 1904.
(Telegraphic.)

Younghusband, telegraphing on 31st March, reports as follows:-
"Advance was made to-day by our force towards

Guru. I was met by Lhasa General, who asked us to retire to Yatung for negotiations. My reply was that for 15 years we had tried to make a settlement at Yatung, and I had waited in Tibet for eight months. I said that the Amban had lately been informed by me that Mission was going to advance to Gyangtse, and that I was going to-day to Guru. General Macdonald would have to clear a passage for Mission if they opposed us. Thereupon Lhasa General retired and force advanced. I asked General Macdonald to issue orders that, unless Tibetans fired, our troops were not to fire. The advance to Guru is now being continued."

∞◦⦅◯⦆◦∞

From the Viceroy to the Secretary of State for India, dated the 1st April, 1904.
(Telegraphic.)

Younghusband telegraphs, on the 31st March, to fol-lowing effect:-"Some resistance was offered at Guru, but we have occupied the village, and will establish there an advance supply depôt, the force returning here in the evening. Our casualties consisted of only a few wounded, of whom only Candler, the correspondent of the "Daily Mail," is severely hurt; we have none killed. The losses of the Tibetans amount to 300 or more killed and many wounded and prisoners. Amongst the killed are the Lhasa General and another General. The scene of the fighting was a post, which had been recently constructed by them actually on the road; they were surrounded to such a degree that our men were pointing their rifles into the camp over the walls. No violence was used by our men who showed very great self-restraint; O'Connor told the Lhasa General that, if his men would surrender their arms, they would be permitted to retire. This, however, had no effect, and General Macdonald then ordered our men to begin disarming the Tibetans, who resisted and attacked our troops with swords and with firing. We then returned the fire. This result was wholly caused by the complete inability of the Tibetans, even when our troops absolutely surrounded them, to take in the seriousness of the situation."

From the Viceroy to the Secretary of State for India, dated the 1st April, 1904.
(Telegraphic.)

Following telegram received from Macdonald:-

"Thuna, 31st March. I moved to Guru this morning to establish a supply depôt at that place, taking the following force with me: Two guns, No. 7 Mountain Battery, two 7-pounders 8th Gurkhas, one-and-a-half companies Mounted Infantry, three companies 23rd Pioneers, four companies 32nd Pioneers, two companies 8th Gurkhas, machine gun Norfolks, and section Field Hospital. We moved out of Thuna at 8 a.m., the ground being covered with snow, about two inches of which fell last night. Colonel Younghusband accompanied me. When we had moved about four miles across the plain we were met by a deputation of Tibetan leaders, who demanded our retiring to Yatung, and threatened trouble if we advanced. Colonel Younghusband replied that we would proceed to Guru, and asked if they were prepared to oppose us, to which no definite answer was given; Colonel Younghusband accordingly asked me to refrain from firing till fired at. A large number of armed Tibetans, estimated at about 2,000, were observed on a hill jutting out into the plain some four miles short of Guru, where they occupied sangars and a high wall commanding the road. I advanced in attack formation, shouldering the Tibetans off the hill, and outflanking them on the plains, without firing, the troops exercising the greatest restraint. The result was that 1,500 Tibetan troops collected behind the high wall, blocking the road, and refusing to budge. They were informed that they would have to lay down their arms, and an attempt was accordingly made to disarm them, a portion of the reserve being moved up for the purpose. The Lhasa leaders then incited an attack upon us, the Lhasa Depon firing the first shot and the Tibetans firing point blank and charging with swords; they were, however, so hemmed in that they could not make use of their numbers, and after a few minutes were in full retreat under a heavy fire of guns, Maxims and rifles, which caused them heavy loss. The 2nd Mounted Infantry were despatched in pursuit, and the balance of the troops reforming pushed on to Guru. The two eastern Guru villages were evacuated, but the western one was held, and, after being shelled, was taken by the End Mounted Infantry and Gurkhas, the garrison surrendering. This ended the engagement, except that the 1st Mounted Infantry continued the pursuit for some miles further. Our casualties are-Major Wallace Dunlop slightly wounded; Mr. Candler, 'Daily Mail' correspondent, severely wounded, and seven sepoys wounded. The enemy's loss is nearly 500 killed and wounded, and 200 prisoners, all their camp and laggage, about 60 yaks and 30 mules, with 2 gingalls and a large number of matchlocks and swords, together with a few breechloaders, two of which were of Russian make. Amongst the Tibetans killed was the chief Lhasa Depon and the Lama representative of the Gaden Monastry; also one Shigatse Depon, whilst the Phari Depon was captured, severely wounded. Two companies 32nd Pioneers and the 2nd Mounted Infantry are established at Guru, as an advanced post, the remaining troops returning to Tuna by 7 p.m., after a long and trying day, having marched 21 miles and fought two engagements. Fuller details follow. Writing report. All Tibetan wounded have been brought in, and are being attended to."

From the Viceroy to the Secretary of State for India, dated the 4th April, 1904
(Telegraphic.)

Casualties, action Guru, 31st March, with Tibetans, are as follows:–Major Wallace Dunlop, wounded severely, lost two fingers; Candler, dangerously wounded, left hand amputated, besides other serious sword wounds; Native ranks, two wounded severely, eight wounded slightly.

From the Viceroy to the Secretary of State for India, dated the 4th April, 1904.
(Telegraphic.)

Younghusband telegraphs from Thuna on 1st April: "Appears from reports of officers who first approached Tibetan post on road that. Tibetans were just commencing to stream away when Lhasa General rode through them and made them remain. Troops in clearing sangars on hill-side simply made Tibetans move on, but allowed them to retreat without firing. It was when a report was brought to General Macdonald that Tibetans in the post which actually blocks the throughfare were refusing to retreat, though surrounded at point-blank range, that Macdonald and I agreed they must be disarmed.

Lhasa General himself tried to prevent disarmament, and shot sepoy with his revolver. This is believed to have been the first shot. The Lama representative of the Gaden monastery was among the killed. He was the most insolent of three Lamas I saw at Guru in January, and a thorough-going obstructionist. I trust the tremendous punishment they have received will prevent further fighting, and induce them at last to negotiate. The ordinary soldiers were before this only half-hearted, and I doubt if Lhasa authorities will be able to induce them to face us again. We shall advance from here in two or three days."

From the Viceroy to the Secretary of State for India, dated the 5th April, 1904.
(Telegraphic.)

Reconnaissance 2nd April last ascertained 2,000 more Tibetans were blocking Gyangtse road at Hram, but retired to Kalatso hearing Guru defeat. It is believed that Tibetans have retired Gyangtse. All wounded doing well.

From the Viceroy to the Secretary of State for India, dated the 5th April, 1904.
(Telegraphic.)

Younghusband wires from Thuna, 3rd April:-
"I have received despatch from Amban in reply to mine. He says he was most anxious to come and meet me on his first arrival, but Dalai Lama

refused him transport. He now intends to come and meet me as soon as possible In view of Tibetan obstinacy he says there is no help for it but we must go to Gyangtse, though Dalai Lama has written to him that we should go back to Yatung. I have written to Amban giving him short account of fight, saying I shall be in Gyangtse in another week's time and hope to meet him with high Tibetan officials there to make a settlement and prevent further bloodshed."

From the Viceroy to the Secretary of State for India, dated the 5th April, 1904.
(Telegraphic.)

Mission arrived Guru 4th April last without opposition.

From the Viceroy to the Secretary of State for India, dated the 8th April, 1904.
(Telegraphic.)

Following telegram received from Younghusband, dated Guru, 4th April:-
    "Ma, delegate from Amban, in place of Ho, Chao, and Li, arrived here from Lhasa, with request that we should return to Yatung. He says he saw 200 Tibetan troops between here and Gyangtse."

From the Viceroy to the Secretary of State for India, dated the 8th April, 1904.
(Telegraphic.)

Younghusband, telegraphing from Kalatso, on the 6th April reports that a Lhasa Major, who is in hospital there, informed him that at engagement at Guru Tibetans had orders not to fire, but were told that if they retreated, or did not stop us, they would have their throats cut. He believes this is probably correct account. There are no signs of serious opposition between Kalatso and Gyangtse. There are several villages in the neighbourhood of Kalatso whose inhabitants, including women, are now returning to their homes. They are friendly, and are bringing in fodder, on payment.

From the Viceroy to the Secretary of State for India, dated the 8th April, 1904.
(Telegraphic.)

Macdonald moved to Chalu 5th April, established post there, and reached Kalapangko 6th April. Mounted Infantry on reconnaissance discovered about 300 Tibetans at Samuda, 13 miles beyond Kalapangko, who opened fire. No casualties.

From the Viceroy to the Secretary of State for India, dated the 9th April, 1904.
(Telegraphic.)

Macdonald reached Salu 7th April. Enemy retired to position eight miles to the north of Kangma. Tibetan casualties, Samuda: killed, six; wounded, three.

From the Viceroy to the Secretary of State for India, dated the 9th April,
(Telegraphic.)

Younghusband reports Amban delegate Ma who has come to meet us says the property of Generals and Lama killed at Guru has been confiscated by Lhasa Government because of their failure to stop us.

From the Viceroy to the Secretary of State for India, dated the 11th April, 1904.
(Telegraphic.)

Macdonald reached Langma, two miles to the north of Khangma, 9th April. Three thousand enemy, after few shots fired, retired five miles to the north of Changra. No casualties. Enemy reported to be receiving reinforcements from Gyangtse.

From the Viceroy to the Secretary of State for India, dated the 13th April, 1904.

Following from Younghusband, dated Chalu, 13th April:-

> "Gyangtse, 11th, by Chinese couriers. General Macdonald has brought Mission here without loss single man. Tibetans who opposed us highly

demoralised. This valley covered with well-built
hamlets; cultivation everywhere and numerous
trees. Inhabitants mostly fled, but few who remain
say this is on account of heavy demands of their
own Government. News just arrived Tibetans are
fleeing from fort. Two Tibetan generals have left,
and Chinese delegate Ma, with Tibetan Jongpen,
have come in. Ma say Amban will come as soon
as he can arrange with Dalai Lama, and that four
Tibetan delegates of unknown position are on
their way. Jongpen is in great fear, and will
doubtless surrender fort tomorrow."

*From the Viceroy to the Secretary of State for India, dated
the 13th April, 1904.*
(Telegraphic.)

Younghusband has sent a full report of incident at
Guru, of which the following are the principal points.
Younghusband met Lhasa general 1,000 yards from
spot where sangars had been erected by Tibetans, and
in conference with him told him that we did not
want to fight, and would not do so provided that no
opposition were offered, but the Tibetan soldiers must
be removed from position, or our troops would have
to clear a way. Reply of Lhasa general consisted of
familiar appeals that we should withdraw to Yatung.
When the conference had proved abortive
Younghusband asked Macdonald to advance troops,
but to order them not to fire unless fired at by

Tibetans. The troops advanced with perfect discipline, not a shot being fired, though they expected a heavy fire from the sangars at any moment. Great hesitation was shown by Tibetans, but being eventually out-flanked they left the sangars. A party occupying post on plain were an exception, being made to return by Lhasa General, and they declined to leave wall built across road, although surrounded. Younghusband decided, with the concurrence of Macdonald, that the only resource was to disarm them and let them go, and Captain O'Connor, who speaks Tibetan and was on friendly terms with the General, was accordingly sent to inform him that the men would be disarmed. The General received this sullenly, and at first took no action, but when, after a short time, the process of dis-arming began he rushed at a sepoy, and drawing his revolver shot him in the jaw. The Tibetans immedi-ately fired other shots, and a rush was made by their swordsmen. It was not until this moment that the British troops commenced firing. Younghusband adds that he deeply regretted the occurrence, to avoid which he had laboured incessantly. The stubborn hos-tility of the leaders from Lhasa and the ignorance of the Tibetans themselves were entirely responsible for the occurrence. The Tibetans were treated with the utmost consideration as soon as the firing was over; the wounded were collected and cared for, and the prisoners were released. Our entire medical staff was sent out to attend the wounded. We join Younghusband in deploring what has occurred, for we had exhausted every diplomatic effort, and delayed for months, in our desire to avoid it; but we exonerate our troops from all blame, and we consider that exemplary patience and fortitude have been displayed by them in circumstances of unequalled rigour and difficulty, where, with the temperature below zero, and at an elevation at which no fighting has ever before taken place, they have had to be on the watch night and day against assault. Further, the advance without firing a short right up to the position held by 2,000 armed Tibetans involved risk of military disaster to the British force, which they were willing to incur owing to their supreme desire to avoid bloodshed, though they would certainly have been blamed for it. The force arrived at Gyangtse two days ago, and in its unopposed advance are seen the effects of the Guru incident.

From the Secretary of State for India to the Viceroy, dated the 13th April, 1904.
(Telegraphic.)

Your telegram of to-day. Please report number of Tibetans killed and wounded respectively in fighting at Guru.

From the Viceroy to the Secretary of State for India, dated the 14th April, 1904.
(Telegraphic.)

Macdonald, in advance to Gyangtse 10th April, met with strong opposition, estimated number 2,000

Tibetans. The enemy was defeated and dispersed. Enemy's loss was 190 dead, many wounded, 70 prisoners. Our casualties were three wounded. Gyangtse Jongpen visited Macdonald desiring peace. Large numbers of Tibetans reported fleeing toward Shigatse.

From the Viceroy to the Secretary of State for India, dated the 14th April, 1904.
(Telegraphic.)

The word "unopposed" in my telegram of yesterday was based on a telegram from Younghusband making no mention of resistance. The telegram in which Macdonald describes action arrived later. Please therefore delete word.

From the Viceroy to the Secretary of State for India, dated 15th April, 1904.
(Telegraphic.)

Gyangtse surrendered 12th April last. Fort has been occupied by two companies of 32nd Bengal Infantry without opposition.

From the Viceroy to the Secretary of State for India, dated the 15th April, 1904.
(Telegraphic.)

Following telegram received from Younghusband:-
    "Gyangtse, 12th. With surrender of the fort this morning resistance in this part of Tibet is ended.

Neither generals, nor soldiers, nor people have wished to fight. Demeanour of inhabitants is respectful; no scowling looks are seen; they bring in supplies for sale, and their wish is not to fight us, but to escape being commandeered by Lhasa authorities. Attitude of monks here is, of course, submissive, but I cannot, at present say anything regarding their real feelings. The local Chinese are naturally making the most of the situation for their own benefit. The Amban makes no signs of coming to meet me, and I am writing to him an urgent letter expressing my surprise at not finding him here. Two Tibetan members of Council, with two subordinates, are said to be on their way here, but I cannot vouch for the truth of this report. Lhasa authorities are quite silly enough to continue obstruction, but Government may consider Mission absolutely safe, in a fertile valley, full of supplies, and amidst a population certainly not actively hostile to us, and whom I will guarantee we will, in three months time, have thoroughly well disposed. We already have released prisoners of war asking for employment."

From the Viceroy to the Secretary of State for India, dated the 15th April, 1904.
(Telegraphic.)

Your telegram of 13th April. Guru incident. Macdonald's full report just received states total of Tibetans killed, and wounded left on field, 628.

Prisoners, some of whom were slightly wounded, 222, and doubtless a number, slightly wounded, escaped. This includes total casualties during fighting at wall and in subsequent pursuit and attack on Guru village. Tibetans numbered 3,000, of whom 2,000 were actually engaged, half being regular troops.

From the Viceroy to the Secretary of State for India, dated the 22nd April, 1904.
(Telegraphic.)

Following telegram received from Younghusband, dated Gyangtse, 18th April:-"Lhasa delegates, who were reported to have been coming, are of low rank, and since receiving news of fighting have halted on their way to receive orders. Headmen here express willingness to sell supplies, which are beginning to come in regularly. There is every sign of this district quieting down."

From the Secretary of State for India to the Viceroy, dated the 22nd April, 1904.
(Telegraphic.)

Please telegraph any available information regarding sickness and frost-bite among escort since advance to Chumbi.

From the Viceroy to the Secretary of State for India, dated the 23rd April, 1904.
(Telegraphic.)

Macdonald left Gyangtse 20th April last for Chumbi to arrange communications. Two guns and six companies at Gyangtse intrenched.

From the Viceroy to the Secretary of State for India, dated the 24th April, 1904.
(Telegraphic.)

Your telegram of 22nd April. General Macdonald reports deaths up to date:-Combatants, 35; followers and coolies, 45. Frost-bites, approximately, combatants, 61; others, 68. Considering altitude and exceptional severity of winter, mortality and sickness wonderfully low, thanks to liberal supply of warm clothing and extra rations. General health has been fair to good, combatants suffering more than followers owing to night duties. Health of force now good.

From the Viceroy to the Secretary of State for India, dated the 25th April, 1904.
(Telegraphic.)

Following from Younghusband:-

"Gyangtse, 22nd April.-I have received a despatch from Amban in which he says he will certainly arrive here within the next three weeks, that he has insisted on the Tibetans giving him transport, and that they have agreed, and that he has insisted also on competent and trustworthy Tibetan representatives accompanying him. He does not state specifically what representatives will accompanying him, but the official who brought the despatch says that one of the Councillors acting in place of the Councillors imprisoned at Lhasa is coming. This official also says that among the common people at Lhasa there is not much excitement, as they are aware that even if we did go there we would not harm them; but that the Tibetan officials at Lhasa are greatly perturbed, and are begging the Amban to come here and settle the matter. The official saw 700 Tibetan troops about sixty miles from here, and another camp nearer to Lhasa. Excepting these there was no sign of military preparation. The Amban's despatch says that the Lhasa general was the aggressor in the Guru affair, but that my compassion in releasing the prisoners and in caring for the wounded, and my humane motives, have conferred incalculable blessing on Tibet. He says the Dalai Lama is now roused to a sense of our power; but since the former councillors are imprisoned, there are few capable Tibetan officials to negotiate. The Amban adds that he does not speak insincerely. Everything here is very quiet. The general attitude is acceptance of the inevitable, combined with relief at the flight of the oppressive Lhasa officials. Sick and wounded are also coming in to be treated by Wilton. Camp is besieged with Tibetans selling country produce, carpets and trinkets. A daily bazaar is now established outside the camp. To-day 177 Tibetans, mostly women, were selling their goods there. The scene presented was very remarkable and significant-British officers and soldiers, Sikhs, Gurkhas, and Bhutias bargaining away peaceably with their foes of a fortnight ago, and giving the sharp Tibetan traders exorbitant prices for vegetables, eggs, condiments, watches, cigarettes, carpets, trinkets, cotton goods, cooking utensils-even penny whistles. The Tibetans are evidently born traders, and they are already sending to Phari for more goods from India. Two hundred and twenty-three maunds of bhoosa and 560 lbs. barley were also brought to-day for sale to the commissariat by sixteen different villagers."

Other titles in the series

John Profumo and Christine Keeler, 1963

"The story must start with Stephen Ward, aged fifty. The son of a clergymen, by profession he was an osteopath ... his skill was very considerable and he included among his patients many well-known people ...Yet at the same time he was utterly immoral."

The Backdrop

The beginning of the '60s saw the publication of 'Lady Chatterley's Lover' and the dawn of sexual and social liberation as traditional morals began to be questioned and in some instances swept away.

The Book

In spite of the spiralling spate of recent political falls from grace, The Profumo Affair remains the biggest scandal ever to hit British politics. The Minister of War was found to be having an affair with a call girl who had associations with a Russian Naval Officer at the height of the Cold War. There are questions of cover-up, lies told to Parliament, bribery and stories sold to the newspapers. Lord Denning's superbly written report into the scandal describes with astonishment and fascinated revulsion the extraordinary sexual behaviour of the ruling classes. Orgies, naked bathing, sado-masochistic gatherings of the great and good and ministers and judges cavorting in masks are all uncovered.

ISBN 0 11 702402 3

The Loss of the Titanic, 1912

"From 'Mesabe' to 'Titanic' and all east bound ships. Ice report in Latitude 42N to 41.25N; Longitude 49 to 50.30W. Saw much Heavy Pack Ice and a great number of Large Icebergs. Also Field Ice. Weather good. Clear."

The Backdrop

The watchwords were 'bigger, better, faster, more luxurious' as builders of ocean-going vessels strove to outdo each other as they raced to capitalise on a new golden age of travel.

The Book

The story of the sinking of the Titanic, as told by the official enquiry, reveals some remarkable facts which have been lost in popular re-tellings of the story. A ship of the same line, only a few miles away from the Titanic as she sank, should have been able to rescue passengers, so why did this not happen? Readers of this fascinating report will discover that many such questions remain unanswered and that the full story of a tragedy which has entered into popular mythology has by no means been told.

ISBN 0 11 702403 1

Tragedy at Bethnal Green, 1943

"Immediately the alert was sounded a large number of people left their houses in the utmost haste for shelter. A great many were running. Two cinemas at least in the near vicinity disgorged a large number of people and at least three omnibuses set down their passengers outside the shelter."

The Backdrop
The beleaguered East End of London had born much of the brunt of the Blitz but, in 1943, four years into WW2, it seemed that the worst of the bombing was over.

The Book
The new unfinished tube station at Bethnal Green was one of the largest air raid shelters in London. After a warning siren sounded on March 3, 1943, there was a rush to the shelter. By 8.20pm, a matter of minutes after the alarm had sounded, 174 people lay dead, crushed trying to get into the tube station's booking hall. At the official enquiry, questions were asked about the behaviour of certain officials and whether the accident could have been prevented.

ISBN 0 11 702404 X

The Judgement of Nuremberg, 1946

"Efficient and enduring intimidation can only be achieved either by Capital Punishment or by measures by which the relatives of the criminal and the population do not know the fate of the criminal. This aim is achieved when the criminal is transferred to Germany."

The Backdrop

WW2 is over, there is a climate of jubilation and optimism as the Allies look to rebuilding Europe for the future but the perpetrators of Nazi War Crimes have yet to be reckoned with, and the full extent of their atrocities is as yet widely unknown.

The Book

Today, we have lived with the full knowledge of the extent of Nazi atrocities for over half a century and yet they still retain their power to shock. Imagine what it was like as they were being revealed in the full extent of their horror for the first time. In this book the Judges at the Nuremberg Trials take it in turn to describe the indictments handed down to the defendants and their crimes. The entire history, purpose and method of the Nazi party since its foundation in 1918 is revealed and described in chilling detail.

ISBN 0 11 702406 6

The Boer War: Ladysmith and Mafeking, 1900

"4th February – From General Sir. Redfers Buller to Field-Marshall Lord Roberts … I have today received your letter of 26 January. White keeps a stiff upper lip, but some of those under him are desponding. He calculates he has now 7000 effectives. They are eating their horses and have very little else. He expects to be attacked in force this week …"

The Backdrop
The Boer War is often regarded as one of the first truly modern wars, as the British Army, using traditional tactics, came close to being defeated by a Boer force which deployed what was almost a guerrilla strategy in punishing terrain.

The Book
Within weeks of the outbreak of fighting in South Africa, two sections of the British Army were besieged at Ladysmith and Mafeking. Split into two parts, the book begins with despatches describing the losses at Spion Kop on the way to rescue the garrison at Ladysmith, followed by the army report as the siege was lifted. In the second part is Lord Baden Powell's account of the siege of Mafeking and how the soldiers and civilians coped with the hardship and waited for relief to arrive.

ISBN 0 11 702408 2

The British Invasion Tibet: Colonel Younghusband, 1904

"On the 13th January I paid ceremonial visit to the Tibetans at Guru, six miles further down the valley in order that by informal discussion might assure myself of their real attitude. There were present at the interview three monks and one general from Lhasa ... these monks were low-bred persons, insolent, rude and intensely hostile; the generals, on the other hand, were polite and well-bred."

The Backdrop

At the turn of the century, the British Empire was at its height, with its army in the forefront of the mission to bring what it saw as the tremendous civilising benefits of the British way of life to what it regarded as nations still languishing in the dark ages.

The Book

In 1901, a British Missionary Force under the leadership of Colonel Francis Younghusband crossed over the border from British India and invaded Tibet. Younghusband insisted on the presence of the Dalai Lama at meetings to give tribute to the British and their empire. The Dalai Lama merely replied that he must withdraw. Unable to tolerate such an insolent attitude, Younghusband marched forward and inflicted considerable defeats on the Tibetans in several onesided battles.

ISBN 0 11 702409 0